To my friend Robert,

with the hope that
he can find this
~~book~~ interesting.

Best,

Emilio

JOSÉ MARTÍ

José Martí

Images of Memory and Mourning

Emilio Bejel

palgrave
macmillan

First published in 2012 by PALGRAVE MACMILLAN® in the United States—a division of St. Martin's Press LLC, 175 Fifth Avenue, New York, NY 10010.

Where this book is distributed in the UK, Europe and the rest of the world, this is by Palgrave Macmillan, a division of Macmillan Publishers Limited, registered in England, company number 785998, of Houndmills, Basingstoke, Hampshire RG21 6XS.

Palgrave Macmillan is the global academic imprint of the above companies and has companies and representatives throughout the world.

Palgrave® and Macmillan® are registered trademarks in the United States, the United Kingdom, Europe and other countries.

ISBN: 978-0-230-34075-6

Library of Congress Cataloging-in-Publication Data

Bejel, Emilio
    José Martí : images of memory and mourning / Emilio Bejel.
       p. cm.
    Includes bibliographical references and index.
    ISBN 978-0-230-34075-6 (hardback : alk. paper)
      1. Martí, José, 1853–1895—Monuments—Social aspects—Cuba. 2. Martí, José, 1853–1895—Portraits—Social aspects—Cuba. 3. Memorialization—Social aspects—Cuba. 4. Memorials—Social aspects—Cuba. 5. Visual sociology—Cuba. I. Title.

    F1783.M38B35 2012
    972.9106092—dc23

A catalogue record of the book is available from the British Library.

Design by Scribe Inc.

First edition: September 2012

10 9 8 7 6 5 4 3 2 1

Printed in the United States of America.

I dedicate this book to my dear in-laws, James and Virginia Gibbs

CONTENTS

FIGURES

About the Artist

Vicente Dopico-Lerner was born in Havana, Cuba, and has lived in Miami since 1965. He has won numerous awards for his paintings and artworks and has participated in many group and individual fine art expositions. He is one of the most renowned Cuban American artists of our time, and his artistic reputation extends not only to Florida and the United States but also to the Caribbean area. He is the artist of the image of Martí found on the cover of this book.

Acknowledgments

A book of this kind is impossible without the help and support of many people. There are numerous friends and colleagues to whom I owe my deepest thanks for their important contributions to this work.

My first acknowledgment goes to my doctoral student and research assistant Jonathan Dettman, who has been editor, insightful critic, and moral support during four years of the manuscript. Jon is one of the very best intellectual minds I have encountered among my graduate students over the years. His editing skills, his knowledge of Cuban culture, and his critical thinking have been invaluable to me in this process.

During the last intense year of this manuscript, I realized that one of the most daunting tasks was the pragmatic one—deciding which iconographic images I was going to include in the text. The complications in obtaining publication permissions and high-resolution images were at times overwhelming, but I was lucky enough to have the incredible skill and persistence of Jonathan Alcántar, another doctoral student at our graduate program in the Department of Spanish and Portuguese at the University of California–Davis. Jonathan is not only very well versed in technological matters, but he is also a keen scholar of Cuban literature and culture, which was another important aspect of his contribution to this endeavor.

Once Palgrave Macmillan accepted my book proposal, the next step was to determine who could be a good editor and indexer for the manuscript. The issue was quickly resolved when the publisher suggested Cathy Hannabach, a visiting lecturer at the University of Pittsburgh. It happens, almost by chance, that Cathy had been in one of my graduate seminars and had finished her PhD in the Cultural Studies Graduate Group here at UC Davis, and I also served on her dissertation committee. I already knew that Cathy was an extremely intelligent person, but when she began to send me her comments about my manuscript, I realized that she was much more than that: she was a first-class intellectual with an incredible knowledge of critical thinking, gender studies, and film theory. Additionally, she was a sharp editor that could see the slightest contradictions in my writing. I owe her quite a lot regarding the final version of my work, but any weakness in my argument is my own responsibility. Cathy's contract as editor and indexer of my manuscript was funded by the UC Davis

Office of Research and a generous research fellowship from the office of Jessie Ann Owens, Dean of Humanities, Arts and Cultural Studies of UC Davis. I thank Jessie Ann and the Office of Research for this very important financial support.

From Cuba, I received amazing help from Elizabeth Mirabal Llorens and Carlos Velazco, two young journalists and writers who have won literary and scholarly prizes for their works on Cuban literature—including the 2011 Casa de las Américas literary prize for a book on Guillermo Cabrera Infante. Elizabeth and Carlos, whom I met during my visit to the island in December 2010, were incredibly generous with their time. I thank them profusely for their innumerable emails with information about how to contact Cuban painters and artists, their humane approach to my vicissitudes when I was having a difficult time with a particular aspect of the research, and their generous invitation to publish my article on Fernando Pérez's 2010 movie *José Martí: El ojo del canario* in the collection of essays published by Ediciones ICAIC and edited by Carlos Velazco.

Elizabeth and Carlos also put me in contact with Fernando. Fernando wrote me extensive emails answering my questions and commenting on my ideas about his excellent film. I am very grateful for his generosity.

My friend Francisco Morán, poet, scholar, and director of the electronic journal *La Habana Elegante* not only accepted my first article about Martí's iconography ("José Martí: Iconografía y memoria") but made valuable suggestions and comments that improved that piece greatly, and that I later kept in mind when I was writing the manuscript of the present work. Thank you, Francisco.

In agreement with Jorge Camacho and other scholars, one of my assertions in Chapter 4 is that some paintings by Cuban artists of the Special Period (especially some that appeared in 1995) are "heretical" or at least "nonconformist" pictorial representations of Martí. Because of this claim, it was important for me to ask this question to some of the living artists themselves. They all answered that that was not their *intention*, although anyone can interpret their works in his or her own way. My special thanks to Reinerio Tamayo Fonseca not only for answering my questions about one of his paintings (*Me duele Cuba* [Cuba Hurts], 1995) but also for sending me a new version of the painting he finished in December 2011. Unfortunately due to space and manuscript length considerations, I had to limit the number of images and consequently my comments about them, but I had received interesting responses from all the artists I wrote to regarding their intentionality, styles, and artistic objectives. Needless to say, in these cases (and in the case of all the opinions and contributions of the people I acknowledge here) I state emphatically that all the ideas I express in the book are my responsibility and no one else's.

My special thanks to my friend the excellent artist Vicente Dopico-Lerner, who has painted a picture exclusively for the cover of this book. Vicente has done similar things with at least four of my previous books. His incredible artistic abilities make him one of the very best Cuban American painters and artists of our time. I consider him more than a good friend, he is a brother who is always ready to help and contribute to my endeavors.

I cannot close this acknowledgment section without mentioning the enormous contribution to this book by my longtime friend and colleague Ramiro Fernández, with whom I have shared a friendship since our early childhood in Cuba and for decades have shared the same passion for literature, culture, and critical thinking. We talk by phone almost every day discussing all sorts of things, and for years we have compulsively discussed the topic of this project. Such an intense and frequent exchange of ideas makes it impossible for me to do complete justice to his contribution to the ideas of this book, but at the very least I have to acknowledge his extraordinary participation in this project.

Finally, I thank my spouse Greg Gibbs for his love and tenderness toward me for so many years and his patience on the many occasions when I have become obsessed with the seemingly endless research and writing of this book.

INTRODUCTION

WHY DOES JOSÉ MARTÍ STILL SEEM LIKE a demigod to the majority of Cubans? What feelings does his figure evoke? What role does his iconicity play in the Cuban national narrative? These are some of the questions that I examine in this book, which—unlike the long list of panegyrics of Martí's life, work, and image—aims to be a critical reflection on and a critical analysis of the interaction among Martí's visual images, their history, and the mythical memory that has been built up around them. José Martí's importance for Cuban history and Latin American thought from the late nineteenth century until the present has been enormous and undeniable. Despite only living 42 years, he achieved extraordinary stature as a politician, journalist, chronicler, orator, thinker, and poet. One of the main reasons he has been admired and even intensely revered by so many across several generations is that he succeeded in creating an image of his political and personal life, not to mention of his role as hero and martyr, that seems to match his message. In this sense, his popularity is like that of Che Guevara, famous for the perception of purity of his ideals, his bold actions, and for dying in combat at an early age as well as the visual images constructed by and around him.[1]

Martí was born in Havana in 1853 to young Spaniards who had moved to the Cuban capital in the mid-nineteenth century. His father, Mariano Martí Navarro, was first sergeant in the Spanish Army's Artillery Corps and was a harsh but honest man of few economic means. In fact, Mariano and his wife, Leonor Pérez had great financial difficulty raising their eight children, among which José was the eldest and the only boy. Despite his father's participation in the Spanish colonial government that then ruled the island, Martí began his revolutionary activities against the crown at a young age, which led to his imprisonment in 1869. He was sentenced to six years confinement, but his mother's entreaties to the Spanish authorities succeeded in effecting his release from prison at the end of 1870. A month later, in January of 1871, Martí was deported to Spain where he studied law and liberal arts (*filosofía y letras*). In 1874, he graduated as a Licentiate in Civil and Canon Law and Liberal Arts. By the end of the 1870s he had traveled to or lived in several countries, including Spain, France, Mexico, Guatemala, and even Cuba (he was deported once again in 1879). In January of 1880, he moved to New York, where he remained for 15 years, until he went to Cuba in 1895 and was killed in battle in a war that in a good measure he himself had organized.[2]

His written work is so extensive that the 1975 edition of his complete works, published in Havana, contains 27 volumes. Many scholars consider him to be the founder of Modernismo, the first truly Hispano-American literary movement (Jrade 1998; Schulman 1966). Modernismo was a complex and contradictory literary and cultural movement that arose in response to modernity's excessive scientism, commercialism, and technological explosion, associated mostly with industrialized countries but that also began to be felt in Latin America (Jrade 1998; Fernández Retamar 1969).[3] Unlike these modernizing forces, Modernismo highlighted spiritual, poetic, and antibourgeois values. Martí's elevated moral tone and the importance he attributed to political action made him very different from other modernistas—Rubén Darío and Julián del Casal, for example—and his work exhibits a distaste for the extreme wealth and materialism of the rapidly advancing modernization projects of the late nineteenth century. Martí's stance against racism and militarism, along with his concern about US expansionism, make him an extremely relevant figure, even today. But his untimely death in battle was what launched his fame and still gives his memory a sacred character that is difficult to question without facing the vehement opposition of his countless followers.

REREADING THE NATIONAL ICON

In this book, I study the corporeal representations of José Martí and the discourses of power that make it possible for Martí's images to be perceived as icons today. I also analyze the reactions of interested observers —those influenced by the Cuban national narrative—when they come across images of José Martí, the national hero of Cuba. I examine photographs, drawings, paintings, and monuments produced from 1862 to the present, as well as a 2010 film about Martí's childhood and adolescent years. Martí emerges as a national icon at the beginning of Cuba's First Republic in 1902 as a vehicle for the national elite to foster a sense of unity in the midst of political instability. As Lillian Guerra has shown, starting with Cuba's First Republic at the beginning of the twentieth century, Martí's iconicity was used by the Cuban state in a conscious manner and following a process of selection of certain images and repression of others. Actually, as Guerra asserts, the more unstable the country was the more the state resorted to the use of Martí's image to centralize its power (Guerra 2005, 1–21, 113– 18, 255–60). This process continued during subsequent governments, including those of Carlos Prío Socarrás (1948–1952) and Fulgencio Batista (1940–1944; 1952–1958), and reached its zenith during that of Fidel and Raúl Castro (1959–present).

Throughout this book, I attempt to answer not only the motivations and shortcomings of some of the political and ideological struggles that have taken place behind the planning and construction of a few of Martí's iconic monuments, statues, and memorials but what political, aesthetic, psychological, and phenomenological factors have contributed to the enormous success of Martí's image as icon through different and even radically opposed governments and ideological configurations. It seems to me that the theory of the politics of memory, as important as it is regarding the collective memory of national heroes, it is not sufficient to completely understand the enormous success of Martí's devotion among Cubans for over a century. That is why in this book I argue that today's interested observer also experiences a *retrospective reconstruction*[4] of

Martí's image that is an integral part of the intense devotion toward the iconicity of Martí's visual representations and its questionings.

Methodologically, I explore these and other issues by approaching different moments of Martí's life and Cuban history in general, but instead of following a traditional historiographical methodology, my approach comes closer to a meditation on the way memory works. My purpose in this book, then, is not to discover the truth or falseness of this or that political interpretation of Martí's iconography but instead to reread and reremember that these images, rather than reflecting the truth of the past, help create an ideological and emotional effect in the memory of the observer who has been influenced by the Cuban national narrative. What this means for my present analysis is that our concern is not with historiographical truth—with the study of past events as past—but with the present memory in its working of the *retrospective reconstruction* of that past. In agreement with Susannah Radstone, I believe that this is not a simple opposition between historiography and memory, or a simplistic conception of present memory as a utopian opposite of modern history and values, but instead an investigation of "the site within which modernity's equivocations found their most pressing expression" (Radstone 2000b, 5).

For those reasons, rather than thinking about Martí's images as mere representations of Cuban cultural history, we need to look at them as depositories and instruments of state power and ideology, as well as expressions of the reciprocal gaze of the observer. Every Cuban political ideology claims to possess the "truth" regarding Martí's ideas and image. However, the iconic image should not be taken as a neutral object on which an indisputable truth can be articulated. On the contrary, I will stress the reciprocal relationship that can be intuited between the image's subject and today's observer. These images, especially those that are considered icons for the communities to which we belong, are like living beings that speak to us, demanding a whole set of responses and commitments (Mitchell 2006). Throughout this study, therefore, the implied observer is always an *interested* one, influenced by different variations of the Cuban national narrative that has done so much to foster the iconicity of Martí's visual image. Because this observer is familiar with the subject of the images studied, when faced with the images' gaze, he or she responds with an entire complex of identifications, needs, desires, and circumstances that give specific meaning to the national icon.

I also assert that in republican Cuba, a sense of national unity was articulated from a variety of ideological positions and through a diversity of media. This sense of unity was partially based on the use and abuse of the images of Martí's body. Martí's own ideas, naturally, have contributed to this concept of unity. Nevertheless, it is his corporeal image that has been taken as the symbolic figure for the entire construct of *cubanía* (Cubanness)—that is, as a metaphor for the body of the nation. Therefore, the central objective of my work is to critically analyze the many ways in which the image of Martí's body has been used as a metaphor for Cuba's social and political body, along with the varied reactions that we ourselves experience as subjects whose cultural memory has been greatly influenced by Cuba's national narrative.

The national narrative attempts—always unsuccessfully—to ensure that Martí's heroic image is used univocally, and the state institutions make enormous efforts to prevent any deviation from the official interpretation of this iconography as heroic and saintly. In this sense, the institutions of the Cuban state have been very active in trying to affect a specific devotion to Martí that uses his images as instruments of hegemonic control, of making *martianismo* a form of cultural and patriotic common sense that it is very difficult to question. Moreover, the hegemony of the Cuban state depends in great measure on the ways that the national past is represented, and the visual representation of Martí's body as the symbol of the body of the nation is a central device in the construction of that past. Actually, social and political changes and shifting ideological positions necessitate a revision of the way the past is understood. In the final analysis, it is a matter of different and changing power arrangements. This is the main reason, I argue, that what really changes about the idea of Martí according to the different ideologies is not necessarily his indisputable national importance, but the place he occupies within each specific national narrative. In other words, the difference regarding his figure within the diverse ideologies that have dominated the Cuban nation always depends on the way his ideas have been manipulated in favor of this or that social and political position. Instead of immersing in these political debates, my book's point of departure is the idea that *the history that interposes itself between the visual image and the observer's present is never neutral.*

All this means that no single interpretation of Martí's iconography is able to completely control the aporias and contradictions that a critical reading can bring to light. We can critically reread Martí's images due to the fact that they themselves contain the possibility of self-subversion; only through a critical analysis can we be more conscious of their effects on us and acquire agency as members of the human community. Contrary to the claims of the different political positions, these images lack direct— unmediated—access to the memory of a past "truth." In fact, they actually produce a memory block due to their strong impact on the viewer and the consequent false impression that there is no need to analyze them.[5]

This approach is guided by a commitment to the idea that the heroic icon, like the idea of traditional art, is an image originally conceived as sacred and unmediated, while the historical body it represents always retains its potential for alterity.[6] I argue that this is what always happens in the case of Martí's iconic images. For example, upon viewing a photo of Martí, one does not witness the historical moment of the shot (or even the context that produced it) but participates instead in two simultaneous moments: the *past* of the person photographed (via the photo's own indexical status as historical document) and the *present* of the observer (definitely conditioned by the legitimizing discourses of "the national"). The objective is to analyze certain aspects of Martí's iconography with the goal of making explicit the mediations that exist in the act of observing Martí's bodily image and to theorize the possible implications of the relationship between what the biased observer "looks" and what he or she actually "sees." This methodology invites one to reflect on the contradictions that emerge from the aporias implicit in Martí's iconography itself and opens new possibilities of imaging Cuba's past, present, and future.

With this purpose in mind, I take up Andrea Noble's suggestion (based on one of Roland Barthes's key principles) that studying the images of Latin America's national heroes must begin with the idea that the photographic image becomes an act of "counter-memory," because its power to captivate the observer gives the false impression that the image is completely present, not requiring contextualization (Noble 2005, 200–203; Barthes 1980, 91).[7] This happens despite the fact that the icon appears to represent an objective historical fact via an act of recuperative memory that recalls something absent in the moment of observation. But iconic images also function as a synecdoche—that is, photos of historical images produced in a specific and limited context often appear as the representation of an entire political movement or of an extremely complex and heterogeneous occurrence (e.g., the famous photo of Francisco Villa in the presidential seat as the representation of the entire Mexican Revolution[8] or, in this study, the image of Martí's body as the representation of Cuban nationality). It is worth insisting that the synecdochic use of Martí's bodily image, as part of and metaphor for the national whole, reveals a desire to conceptualize the nation as a homogeneous unity. Analyzing this process will require carrying out Noble's proposal that first we must return those images to the historical flow and, in so doing, overcome or problematize the historical amnesia engendered by the observation of the images themselves (Noble 2005, 206–7). This first step serves two purposes: to anchor the iconic image in history and, at the same time, destabilize the mythical process—implicit in the nature of the icon—by returning it to the contingency of historical time. Here one can bring to bear one of Stuart Hall's ideas, according to whom "myths concentrate and condense; histories disperse and de-center," which points toward a methodology that, while taking into consideration the process of remembering, interrogates myths by referring them primarily to history in order to reconstruct the effect that the iconic image produces (Hall 2003, 481). As mentioned before, the historical flow named here is more concerned with the process of memory than with history in any objective sense. The analysis of iconic images must take into account the fact that certain images function essentially like a retrospective salvage operation in which memory is contingent on a process in which particular images are selected, and others rejected, according to the needs of the national narrative (Noble 2005, 209). This process clearly implies that more than the historical event itself, what determines the way in which the viewer observes and reads these images is nothing other than the ideological and emotional baggage shaping the nation as an "imagined community" (Anderson 1983).

Here the workings of memory are considered as acts of reconstructing or re-membering the national body. In this regard, we should recall Noble's assertion that "the contemporary turn to memory is arguably a more productive approach to the historical freight of the iconic photograph" (Noble 2005, 203). In her insightful *Memory and Methodology*, Susannah Radstone proposes that the recent interdisciplinary interest in memory is due at least partly to the postmodernist rejection of modernity's blind faith in futurity, progress, and objectivity. Memory, in its workings, deals with matters of subjectivity and its consequent micronarratives of the private realm (Radstone 2000a, 3). This foregrounds memory's status as representation, which in turn highlights processes of selection, condensation, repression, displacement, and rejection (Noble 2005, 203). These processes result in a collection of fragments that behave as a palimpsest rather than as a coherent whole. This is a process of deferred revision —which, far from resulting in a faithful memory, is a reinvention of the past based in great measure on the observer's present needs. Here, it is useful to bring up the ideas of Nancy Wood, who follows Maurice Halbwachs in distinguishing collective memory from that of the individual: "What differentiates these two modes of memory is that while emanations of individual memory is primarily subject to the laws of the unconscious, public memory—whatever its unconscious vicissitudes—testifies to a will or desire on the part of some social group or disposition of power to select and organize representations of the past so that these will be embraced by individuals as their own. If particular representations of the past have an intentionality—social, political, institutional and so on—that promotes or authorizes their entry" (Wood 1999, 2).

Taking the ideas discussed so far into consideration, we can say that Martí's iconography does not give us access to any "historical truth" but instead creates a memory block that only a critical methodology can make obvious. Returning a given image to the historical flow and critically analyzing it enable us to subvert, or at least question, the discourses of power that have constructed the ideas and emotions that Martí's iconography produces in the national imagination. In other words, this book's methodology attempts to foster a greater consciousness of the effects that Martí's iconography has on the observer who has been influenced by the Cuban national narrative. I also aim to show how certain representations of Martí correspond to different views of Cuba and its national hero. My approach is an attempt to challenge the hegemonic discursive structures that have constructed and disseminated these images, and I also hope to reveal how this construction and dissemination, if examined from a critical perspective, point toward the destabilization of the hegemonic discourses that formed them. What remains of Martí in his portraits? Why do they still fascinate us across so much time and space? One answer to these questions is that in addition to the manipulations carried out by national elites, there must be more phenomenological and psychological elements that explain the elevation of Martí's visual image to the status of icon.

Iconographic images always appear represented in what W. J. T. Mitchell calls "mixed media." We cannot forget, then, that Martí's images often appear inserted into historical and school texts or alongside anthems, speeches, and flags. On the other hand, as Mitchell proposes, all representations are already *mixed* because even a written text is already visual, since when we read we also form visual images of what the text suggests to us (Mitchell 2005). Mitchell's ideas lead us to consider the fact that the visual image forms part of the structure of the written text and that there is a cross-contamination between image and language. On this basis we can also conclude that, as is the case in other situations of identity and alterity, the image—constructed as writing's and conceptual's other—tends to return, in times of crisis, to the surface of consciousness as the repressed element of language.[9]

This book also considers the feelings of mourning and melancholia, particularly as they are attached to the death of the vanished hero, which is an integral part of the Cuban national discourse and its sense of patriotism. This is particularly obvious when one deals with photos of the martyr-hero, because when a photo is taken of the real Martí, the camera simultaneously captures an image of the person and attempts to give it graphic expression, transporting it—like death does—from a real temporality to an immobile and silent one. Additionally, Martí's iconography is often associated with an almost-religious martyrdom whose characteristics are indisputably similar to the martyrdom of Christ (Guerra 2005, 117). All this forms part of the Cuban national narrative, which—in addition to its purely political motives—constructs a discourse of heroism and martyrdom that is both a kind of unresolved mourning for the vanished hero and an icon of resurrection that demands a particular behavior from the country's citizens. The national elite of every political tendency, in addition to constructing such a heroic-religious discourse, makes efforts to identify itself with Martí's ideals. But it is here where one of the greatest aporia resides: the construct is always victim of contingency and disillusion because, in the end—from a demystifying perspective—the hero is not alive, nor does he live on in the Cuban citizens.

If Walter Benjamin's influential essay "The Work of Art in the Age of Mechanical Reproduction" is to be taken literally in the sense that the advent of photography diminished the "aura" of art due to the reproducibility of the photographic image, and if we relate Martí's iconicity with the aura of his photos, we might conclude that the aura of the latter, its magic, has been diminished by their massive reproduction and dissemination (Benjamin 1969b). But we should take into consideration that in his later writings on photography (in "A Short History of Photography," for example), Benjamin himself proposes an alternative concept of the aura that is relevant to the study of Martí's images and their effects (Benjamin 1980). Benjamin describes a model based on what Carolin Duttlinger calls "imaginary encounters" between the observer and the image (Duttlinger 2008). Following this model, the aura of Martí's photos does not depend entirely on a mechanically historicist or technological conception but on the distance established between observer and observed and the seduction that the observer experiences in his or her perception of the represented subject's gaze. In the final analysis, this is a concept that can be associated with Barthes's notion of the *punctum* of a disappeared loved one's photo.[10] Many observers who look at the iconic photos of Martí establish a reciprocal relationship in which there is simultaneously a certain awareness of distance and absence and also a temporary erasure of the distance between the image and the observer. This is an unconscious game of presence and absence, of the Freudian Fort/Da, and it is precisely here where the captivating power of Martí's image resides. For all these reasons, I propose that what has often occurred with Martí's iconic images is the reverse of a diminished aura or magic: the phenomenological qualities of the images, combined with their political manipulation and the wanting produced by the unresolved sense of mourning for the loss of the martyr-hero, are themselves the elements that contribute to the mystique, or aura, that surrounds Martí.

This approach reflects a conviction that such a critical exercise is especially relevant in a moment like the present in which there has been an explosion of interdisciplinary interest in the role of memory (starting around the 1980s) as a *retrospective reconstruction* that questions some of modernity's fundamental beliefs. Thus analyzing the relationship between iconography and the state is a way of repoliticizing the practice of Latin American cultural studies, extending it beyond the "lettered city."[11] This is an attempt to recall and re-member Martí's symbolic body in order to create a fresh-eyed interpretation of the national body at a moment in which Cuba might be entering a new stage of its history given the social and economic changes that are taking place in the island since Raúl Castro assumed the presidency of the country.

Therefore, the main objective of this type of critical inquiry is to use the analysis of Martí's visual images as a means to question dominant and undertheorized structures and practices of power. The function of this criticism points to the possibility of social and political agency that can be acquired when we increase our critical sophistication as rational and sentient people who can think and feel in new ways about the social and political universe (Wells 2003, 3). But what are these new ways? This book advocates a questioning of the modern Cuban nation's ideas about the iconicity of Martí's visual representations (with implications for the iconicity of other national heroes elsewhere), and explores how this questioning may suggest a renewed cultural and political map in our time (Jameson 1988). It is my hope that this approach to Martí's iconicity can renew our understanding of the memory of the Cuban martyr-hero in such a way that we acquire a new cultural and political cartography of where we are as citizens of the globalized world in which we live and our connection to Cuba's past, present, and future history.

A BRIEF CHAPTER SUMMARY

Chapter 1, "Gaze, Intentionality, and Manipulation," begins by establishing the ideological subtext of Martí's ambivalent and paradoxical position regarding the new technological changes of his time and the similarities and differences between his position and those of Karl Marx, Friedrich Engels, and Walter Benjamin. Then, in the second section of the chapter, I examine Martí's first portrait, taken in 1862 when he was nine years old, and develop the idea of the *reciprocal gaze* between observer and observed. Here, I argue that the mournful eyes of the young Martí focus a gaze that can be viewed as salvaging the magic or aura of the individual subject from the conventions and constrictions of the serial reproduction of photography in the later part of the nineteenth century. This suggests that the process of *reciprocal gaze* is a form of momentary interruption that permits the possibility of subjective agency or at least a brief break from the hegemony that constrains the social and emotional effect of modern life as perceived by the interested observer of the photo. It is an instant space that goes beyond what Benjamin called the homogeneous empty time of the capitalist present (Radstone 2000b, 3; Huyssen 1995, 6). The third section deals with the intentionality and manipulations of Martí's photos from 1870 (the date of his photo in jail) to 1894 (one of Martí's last picture during his life and before his death the following year). Finally, in the fourth section I argue, following Ottmar Ette, that the year 1891 is of utmost importance because it was then that Martí arrived at a crucial stage of his preparation for Cuba's last war of independence, and he became progressively more conscious of the visual image he wanted to project of himself. This explains the fact that the bust portraits of Martí that appeared in and beyond 1891 are those that are now considered his most iconic (Ette 1994, 254). All this shows that Martí himself initiated the manipulation of his own visual image, and thus he was an active participant in the construction of the national narrative that forms our social memory at the present time.

In Chapter 2, "Battling for the National Icon," I focus on statues, memorials, and monuments from 1902 (the beginning of the First Republic) to the present. In all the sections of this chapter, I argue that monuments try to overcome their own ontological instability by inscribing images in stone, marble, or bronze in an attempt to halt the dispersion of heroic meaning implied in those icons. I also analyze here the political and ideological struggles that have taken place behind the planning and construction of some of Martí's best-known iconic monuments. Also, I discuss in this chapter some of the diverse dominant images of Martí promoted by state institutions from 1902 to the present, and how much they depend on the political objectives of the national elite of the moment. In my opinion, these struggles show the contradictions of the official idealized views about Martí behind what the statues, memorials, and monuments, as well as the rituals and celebrations around them, are supposed to represent. But my main theoretical objective in this chapter is to establish the relationship between the individual sense of mourning for the martyr-hero and the use and manipulation of that feeling at the collective level by state and pressure groups interests as part of the Cuban national narrative.

Chapter 3, "The Filming of a Memory," analyzes Fernando Pérez's 2010 film *José Martí: El ojo del canario* (José Martí: The Eye of the Canary) and establishes connections between the photographic images of Martí's youth and their cinematographic representations. The relationships between the still photographic images of Martí and the moving images representing him in the film leads me to conclude that the film as a medium repeatedly plays with the slippage between the moving film image and the static photo image of Martí—that the interested observer carries in her/his memory—and vice versa. This reciprocal movement prevents us from completely accepting the intimate relationship between the photo and death. In conclusion, this means that the gaze of Martí's photographic still image implies the search for a moving image that imitates life, while the moving images of the film seek to immortalize the national hero in a kind of photographical stillness. This is the complex dynamic of melancholia behind the feeling that Martí's admirers are overcome with when they see this film with the memory of his photographs in the back of their minds.

In Chapter 4, "Melancholia for Martí," I focus on a shot of Martí's skull taken a few days after he was killed in Dos Ríos in 1895, as well as on a movie, a painting, and some drawings related with Martí's death. I argue that these images are evocative of what I perceive as the melancholic meaning for Martí's death within the Cuban national imagination. The compulsive reproduction of his image within Cuban culture is but one example of what seems as melancholia for the loss of the martyr-hero, for the trauma of his untimely death and the vacuum that his loss left in a holistic sense of Cuban national narrative. That is obviously why the cult of Martí implies that the hero's body must be revived within a kind of imagined history or redemptive teleology, but a hidden feeling of unresolved mourning, of melancholia, seems to remain. This chapter explores that feeling through some images related with Martí's death. In this chapter I also trace the importance of the year 1995 for the study of Martí's iconography. This year marks the centenary of Martí's death and the appearance, in the so called Special Period,[12] of several paintings by young Cuban artists who, intentionally or not, begin to create partially desacralized images of Martí (Camacho 2003). The "heretical" paintings from those years present a basic paradox: while official state policy during this period increases its dedication to an ideologically favorable vision of Martí's iconography in support of the regime, it is in precisely at this same moment that some plastic artists give their work on Martí's image heretical nuances. I ask myself here whether this phenomenon is an artistic glimpse of a new special insight in Martí's iconicity and a step toward a partial liberation from the Cuban melancholia for the national martyr-hero.

For most Cubans and other interested observers, Martí's memory continues to be the most believable, most sincere, and most self-sacrificing martyr, and perhaps for that reason we are so willing to let ourselves be carried along by a reciprocal gaze that connects his image with our present condition. It will be interesting to see what role Martí's iconography plays in future historical stages, what new discourses will penetrate it, and what importance it will have for an age in which images seem—given the rise of cybernetic experiences and the new possibilities for digital imagery and social media—to delegitimize older truth postulates.

CHAPTER 1

Gaze, Intentionality, and Manipulation

Modern Times, New Technology

In this chapter I will use a variety of discursive strategies to answer what the relation is between the specific characteristics of José Martí's photos and the photographic medium as typically employed during this period. It should be noted that on Sunday, January 3, 1841, thanks to George Washington Halsey, Cuba became the second country in the world and the first in Hispanic America to open a public or commercial daguerreotype studio.[1] The prediction later made by José Martí in 1885 that "photographers will populate the world!"[2] was thus something less than a visionary prophecy since by 1839, more than a decade before his birth, a veritable explosion of enthusiasm for the new daguerreotype technology had begun in Havana. The constant exchange of daguerreotypists among Havana, Paris, and New York was spectacular during these years, and a number of businesses devoted to the daguerreotype also emerged. Several daguerreotypists from the United States, Canada, Italy, England, Spain, France, and Cuba itself participated in the process of invention and commercialization of the daguerreotype in Havana. This period was when Louis Daguerre's machine began to be perfected to the point that three-minute shots were made possible, and the evolution of the procedure was such that by the mid-1850s, although it was called "daguerreotype on paper," what was happening in Cuba and some other countries was in fact photography, complete with the power of large-scale reproduction (Del Valle 2004–5, 4–15; Del Valle 2009, 1–6). This historic situation leads us to a question that guides this chapter: what is the relationship between the historic phenomenon of photography in general and Martí's iconography in particular?

I bring up this information in order to establish certain historical and ideological basis for the relationship between Martí's photographic images and the invention of photography. The fact that Martí was born during the age of photography's rise should be highlighted because of the intimate relationship between his ideas on literary style and the new technological inventions, especially photography. It is not difficult to argue, then, that the success of Martí's iconicity has been influenced by the fact that he was born precisely in the apogee of photography. After all, as Julio Ramos has articulated, one of Martí's main contributions as politician and thinker was his enormous effort to find a place for the new Latin American intellectual in the midst of nineteenth century's explosion of scientism and new technologies (Ramos 1989, 145–243). As an adult residing in New York in 1881, he wrote enthusiastically and in detail about the invention of photography:

> It was an enormous advance to succeed in affixing images obtained in the camera obscura, but it is no less certain that man has not contented himself with all the advances achieved by photography. For nearly a half century the affixation of colors, that is, the obtention of images with their own coloration, has likewise been sought tirelessly. This great invention, whose achievement has been announced repeatedly, but never produced, seems finally resolved by a procedure devised by Messrs. Cros and Carpentier, who just presented, to the Paris Academy of Sciences, photographs of a watercolor, in which the details and colors of the original are reproduced exactly. They were produced on photographs by way of three gravures for each object; gravures obtained respectively through three liquid diaphragms, one orange, one green, and one violet. The opacity and transparency vary from one gravure to another on homologous sections of the image, in order to distribute the relative quantities of red, yellow, and blue (which are the primary colors that form all of nature's hues), so that all of the model's shades are composed and reproduced. Once the layer of sensitive collodion is applied to the paper or glass, in order to obtain the negative proofs, it

is soaked in ammonium dichromate and then dried on the stove. [. . .] With this method it is easy to obtain photographic images in every color. To do so, it is necessary to repeat the operation three times on a single pane of glass, employing a bath of red colorant for the imaged obtained with the green diaphragm, a yellow bath for the orange diaphragm, and finally a yellow bath for the violet diaphragm. It will be truly magical to obtain photographs in which the exact copy of nature's lines is united with the vibrancy and animation of color.[3]

In spite of his obvious enthusiasm for photography's capacity to render detail and the process of obtaining color prints, Martí was never really satisfied with what he thought of as the moral, aesthetic, and political consequences of the era's new technology. His opinion about what was happening at that time was often ambivalent and paradoxical, and sometimes he turned his pen toward a harsh criticism of modernization. Only a few months (1882) after the previous note was written, Martí penned a long prologue to Venezuelan poet Juan Antonio Pérez Bonalde's "Poema del Niágara" (Niagara's Poem) in which he reflects on the negative effects of modernity on art and people's lives: "Contemptible times, these: when the only art that prevails is that of piling one's own granaries high, sitting on a seat of gold and living all in gold, without perceiving that human nature will never vary and the only result of digging up external gold is to live without gold inside! Contemptible times: when the love and exercise of greatness is a rare and outmoded quality. [. . .] Contemptible times: when the priests no longer deserve the praise or reverence of the poets, but the poets have not yet begun to be priests!"[4]

As it is easy to ascertain from the previous piece, Martí is expressing a very strong rejection to what he saw as some of the salient characteristics of his time: greed and lack of respect for an art free from material profit; in other words, art independent of the market. And Martí also references, in this same text, the crisis of poetry and contemporary society: "Trains vanquish the wilderness; newspapers, the human wilderness. [. . .] All is expansion, communication, florescence, contagion, diffusion. [. . .] If spiritual freedom is not safeguarded, then literary originality has no place and political freedom does not long endure. Man first task is to reconquer himself. [. . .] Only what is genuine is fruitful. Only what is direct is powerful."[5]

This commentary reveals that Martí is reacting to the period of modernization in which he happens to live. It was an age in which the new and dynamic forces of capitalism drove technological inventions like photography that greatly influenced the period's art and, as an opposite reaction to those modern technologies, the doctrine of "art for art's sake" and the Hispano-American Modernismo, which several critics believe was founded by Martí (Jrade 1998). If Modernismo was an attempt to achieve a sophisticated style that sought uniqueness and avoidance of the possibility of repetition of individual works of art, the new technologies—photography in particular—made reproduction of its product as one of its greatest achievements (Jameson 1988, 347–57).

From our twenty-first-century vantage point, it is hard to avoid the conclusion that Martí's opinions were a modernist reaction to a world that was changing at a breakneck pace, moving toward a new way of seeing art, artists, culture, society, and even reality itself (Ramos 1989, 7–16, 145–243). Also, Martí, like many other thinkers of his time, was concerned about the growing commercialization of any cultural artifact that could be reproduced en masse, the resulting importance of acquiring wealth through these reproduction processes, and the abuse of the workers who provided the labor power that created industrial products. In my opinion, in this respect, Martí has unintended similar ideas as thinkers like Karl Marx, Friedrich Engels, and Walter Benjamin with whom one sees a conflicting discussion: on one hand, the democratizing power (because of its massive reproduction and dissemination) of new technologies like photography; and, on the other, the transformation of their products into commodities that appeared to destroy the humanistic values that these thinkers considered positive. Specifically regarding art, what Martí, Marx, and Engels (and later Benjamin) feared was the fetishization of the aesthetic produced by the mechanical reproducibility of images and art, and their transformation into commodities. Photography, in this sense, could end up less of an art than an industry (Mitchell 2003).

This explains both the Marxist fascination with photography and cinema's possibility of democratizing art, and its ambivalence toward these same inventions for their proclivity to become mainly an industry. Something similar occurs with Martí, although there are fundamental differences between his position and that of classical Marxism, as I will explain with a brief discussion of some of Benjamin's ideas regarding photography and the connection I see with Martí's position. Benjamin, in his essays on photography (which, according to W. J. T. Mitchell are the most advanced expression of Marxist ambivalence regarding photography and art in general), considers the photographic camera the greatest expression of capitalist consumerism, a consumerism that causes the weakening and even the disappearance of the "aura" or magic of artworks and, in the end, of all reality due to its reification and "flattening" of every cultural artifact (Mitchell 2003). Benjamin's idea about the camera's effect on the visual world corresponds to what Marx had already said about capitalism's effects on social and economic life in general (Benjamin 1969b; Mitchell 2003). But the main difference between the Marxist conception and Martí's ideas is rooted in Marxism's great confidence in the revolutionary power of the dialectical inversion of these evils. According to classic Marxism, capitalism will reach a limit that will reveal its own contradictions, and this situation will cause the new class (the proletariat) to become aware of its dispossession and forced to complete the inevitable revolution (Benjamin 1969b; Benjamin 1999; Mitchell 2003). As an extension of this idea, Benjamin considered the photographic camera (due to its capacity to reproduce images that can be sold in the market) as both the material incarnation of capitalist ideology and a symbol of the process that will result in the end of ideology—given precisely to the possibility of the camera to take to the limit the reproducibility of images until making obvious capitalist contradictions (Benjamin 1969b; Benjamin 1999). Martí's position, however, includes neither class struggle nor the end of ideology in a classless society. In an 1883 eulogy to Marx, Martí writes,

> He [Karl Marx] deserves to be honored for declaring himself on the side of the weak. But the virtuous man is not the one who points out the damage and burns with generous anxiety to put it right; he is one who teaches a gentle amendment of the injury.
>
> The task of setting men in opposition against men is frightening. The compulsory brutalization of men for the profit of others stirs anger. But an outlet must be found for this anger, so that the brutality cease before it overflows and terrifies. [. . .] Labor beautifies: it is rejuvenating to see a farmworker, a blacksmith, or a seaman. By manipulating the forces of Nature, they become as beautiful as Nature is.
>
> Karl Marx is named [in the assembly in his honor that Martí attended] the most noble hero and most powerful thinker of the world of labor. Music sounds; choirs resound; but note that these are not the sounds of peace. (Martí 1975b. Also published in *La Nación* [Buenos Aires], May13 and 16, 1883. Dated New York, March 29, 1883.)

As this shows, Martí—although ambivalent about capitalist modernization and scornful of excessive wealth and abuses against the proletariat—strongly disagreed with the idea that class struggle was the way to confront the evils of the age. We can deduce, therefore, that his ambivalence about the effects of new technology did not imply that he thought a moment would arrive in which a society without ideology would result from the working class's seizure of power. Martí's solution was much more modest and considerably less categorical than that of classical Marxism. His ideas were based on a personal conviction of possible harmony and understanding among human beings. This is the area of Martí's philosophy that connects him with a form of liberal humanism, and clearly distances it from Marxism. In my opinion, due to their lack of realism, Martí's ideas about a possible harmony among all people without some kind of revolution today may seem just as inadequate as the Marxist ones do, although for very different reasons.[6]

THE RECIPROCAL GAZE

As mentioned in the preceding section, by the last half of the nineteenth century Havana had become an important center of daguerreotype, photography studios, and galleries; and the Cuban capital produced a considerable variety of photographic formats and procedures. Additionally, personal portraiture quickly became—in Cuba as elsewhere—an almost obligatory way for the nobility and nascent bourgeoisie to capture their images. But Martí's poetry—indeed, all of his work—can be taken as an ambivalent and ultimately antagonistic response to late nineteenth-century modernization and compulsive urbanization, mass culture (recall Martí's reaction to Coney Island; Martí 1975a), and phenomenal technological advances. I argue, then, that Martí's ambivalent resistance to modernization is reflected not only in his writing and speeches but also in the way his ideas gradually approached the characteristics he preferred for his visual representations. In other words, as I will explain in detail in what follows, Martí, as he became progressively aware of his role as leader, not only of Cuban independence but also of a modernista view of the world, insisted to control his photographic image as a way to project the idea of humbleness and simplicity, which was the opposite of the characteristics of what bourgeois photography was rapidly becoming at the end of the nineteenth century.

In 1851, the Catalan Esteban Mestre photo gallery was established on Havana's O'Reilly Street (Quesada y Miranda 1985, 8). This establishment, which operated for thirty years, was where the nine-year-old José Martí was first photographed (this is his first known photo, at any rate).

In this studio photo we see Martí as a young boy in 1862, posing in Mestre's gallery with the medal he received for his outstanding grades in English. As interested observers greatly influenced by the Cuban national narrative today, what sort of instinctive curiosity do we feel when we see the eyes of the young boy? First, we might ask ourselves what that boy, who would later become such an important figure in Cuban and Latin American history, might

Figure 1.1   Nine-year-old José Martí, 1862

Gonzalo de Quesada y Miranda describes the photograph as such: "First known picture of Martí from his school years. The medal corresponds to a prize for his outstanding performance in the English classes at the San Anacleto School belonging to Rafael Sixto Casado. There is a copy of this photograph at the *Biblioteca Nacional José Martí*, in Havana, given on July 12, 1902, to Domingo Figarola-Caneda, first director of the National Library, by a hairdresser named Enrique Bermúdez. Martí, as a boy, used to accompany Bermúdez when the latter went to work at the theaters, and in that way Martí was able to attend to the shows. Another copy was sent by Martí's mother, Leonor Pérez, to Marcelina de Aguirre, Martí's godmother, who wrote on the back of the photo: '*José Martí was born in Havana, was his godmother Mrs. Marcelina de Aguirre.*' This picture also has imprinted a crown between two bouquets of flowers and the inscription: '*E. Mestre—Photographer with Royal Privilege—O'Reilly 63—Havana.*'"[7]

have been thinking and feeling at the time of the shot. The photo possesses a trace of the past, of a concrete moment. Its status today, as it arrives to us laden with the discourses of power that made Martí into a national and even hemispheric icon, makes us aware of the temporal and spatial distance between us in the present and the subject of the portrait in the past. It also erases or clouds those same distances by virtue of its emotionally encircling impact that now fills those of us under the influence of the Cuban national narrative with a feeling of melancholic empathy (Barthes proposes that the visual impact of the visual image, especially that of a loved one, is always "violent").[8] This is one of Martí's visual images to become a national icon in Cuba. The mental game played by the viewer is formed from a dynamic between the past and present, absence and presence, based on the principle of the reciprocal gaze between the observer and the subject of the portrait. In his "Little History of Photography," Benjamin proposes the following about this very phenomenon: "Immerse yourself in such a picture long enough and you will realize to what extent opposites touch, here too: the most precise technology can give its products a magical value, such as a painted picture can never again have for us. No matter how artful the photographer, no matter how carefully posed his subject, the beholder feels an irresistible compulsion [*Zwang*] to search such a picture for a tiny spark of contingency, of the here and now, with which reality has (so to speak) seared the subject" (Benjamin 1999b, 510).

In "On Some Motifs in Baudelaire," he adds,

What was inevitably felt to be inhuman, one might even say deadly, in daguerreotype was the (prolonged) looking into the camera, since the camera records our likeness without returning our gaze. But looking at someone carries the implicit expectation that our look will be returned by the object of our gaze. Where this expectation is met [. . .], there is an experience of the aura to the fullest extent. [. . .] Experience of the aura thus rests on the relationship between the inanimate or natural object and man. The person we look at, or who feels he is being looked at, looks at us in turn. To perceive the aura of an object we look at means to invest it with the ability to look at us in return. (Benjamin 1969a, 187–88)

Following Benjamin's suggestion, we can say that in Martí's 1862 photo, it is not difficult for an interested observer influenced by the Cuban national narrative to perceive the sad eyes of an intense nine-year-old boy who seems somehow uncomfortable—perhaps due to the suffocating ambience of the studio and the specific contrived pose that he undoubtedly was asked to take. Therefore, we can see that it is in the *reciprocal gaze* between the sad-looking boy of the picture and the interested observer where the seduction of this image seems to reside.

For an interested observer—again, I refer mostly to a Cuban or someone under the influence of the Cuban national narrative— what seems most seductive about the 1862 photo is the boy's sad, startled look, which distances him from the normativity of the era's studio conventions (i.e., the elegant suit, the medal, and the static and contrived pose of the 1862 photo). In this sense, the gallery and its conventions that surround the subject are the *studium*, and the boy's expression represents the *punctum* or detail that marks the individuality and contingency of the image (Barthes 1980). This means that as observers (influenced by the Cuban national narrative), we participate, by looking at this photo, in a complex tension between the period's conventions and the subject's individual resistance to them and our own empathetic reaction to the boy's gaze. When we look at the subject of this portrait, we are involved in an activity that mixes technological matters (pertaining to the period): the subject's individual reaction to being photographed (which seems to resist the demands and norms of the new invention) and our intellectual and emotional reaction to seeing the startled young boy. All this adds up to a complex relation between us and the image that simultaneously unites (via empathy) and separates (by time and distance). Both the observers and the observed participate simultaneously in the complexity of modernization, in its (in)conveniences and conventions, and also in rejecting the attractive but suffocating turn-of-the-nineteenth-century world and its relationship to the observer's present. In a sense, looking at the portrait establishes a reciprocal dialogue between observer and observed and, again, the boy's startled and sad eyes are where the magic (Benjamin would call it *aura*) of the photo is concentrated.[9]

This reflection on the portrait leads me to elaborate further on the epochal consequences of such a *reciprocal gaze*. It must be clarified from the outset that this exchange implies, not an ahistorical response but an imaginary, empathetic relationship between the gaze of the portrait's subject and the interested observer's reaction to it. The reciprocal gaze appears as the desire to overcome the reification of modernity (generally) and photographic conventions (particularly). Additionally, this dynamic means that the photographic image of a dead loved one possesses a certain morbid silence and immobility. The magic of the boy's image ultimately depends not only on the observer's subjective capacity for allowing the image to return his or her gaze but also on the awareness that the photo's subject is dead and gone. In this situation the photograph captures a moment of real life in the past and transports it to another kind of reality, a graphic reality that tries to make us believe for a moment that we are seeing something with an active presence. In this imaginary relationship, what is important is the reciprocal dynamic of gazing, along with the necessary retrospective reconstruction that establishes an emotional connection between the observer and the observed. Such a connection acquires its meaning through the mediation of the discourses of power that saturate both the image and the individual emotional experience of the observer. In the final analysis, this experience is both collective and individual. Moreover, in Benjaminian terms, this reciprocal gaze entails a certain *auratic* (magical) expression in an age that begins to be *postauratic* (critically modern), an age that is thought to have lost its quasi-religious capacity for revering things as sacred, original, magical, or unique.

INTENTIONALITY AND MANIPULATION

As an adult, Martí insisted on having himself portrayed in certain ways, as he became progressively aware of the world he lived in and the position he was carving out for himself within it. In his Madrid portrait (Figure 1.2), probably taken in 1871, a year after his initial deportation, the young Martí appears impeccably dressed, and in a fashionable pose.

From what we could characterize as an objective or naive perspective, it is hard to imagine from this photo the other iconic Martí—the one who later became the martyr, the apostle, and the national hero of Cuba. This photo shows a Martí who looks like a dandy of the era, elegantly dressed and in a pose that was typical of refined people of the time. If we do not consider everything that occurred before and after the photo was taken, and if we did not know about what has subsequently been said and written about Martí as well as seen the other iconic pictures of him, we would see something completely different from what we *do* see today— that is, the interested observer sees in this picture the future leader of the Cuban national independence. All this shows how history always inserts itself into the images we see and what we know about them in advance.

In Martí's specific case, these are images laden with national discourses of power, which are characterized not only by their attempt to inculcate a univocal view of interpreting Martí's iconography but also by the way they erase the historical context that produced the iconic images. That is, although it might seem that looking at a photograph of Martí makes his image and history visible to us, we are really participating in a double operation of invisibility: history is often blurred by the impact of the photographic image—its visual effect is so overwhelming that it clouds our ability to reflect on it—and the image itself, which we believe to be an objective, biographical document, actually hides its nature as a semiotic complex of discourses of power.

Martí's iconic images form part of a Cuban national teleology, one of whose pillars is constructed precisely from these same

Figure 1.2   Dandy José Martí, 1871*

"Photo of Martí probably taken in Madrid during his first deportation. It appeared published in a leaflet distributed by the newspaper *Cuba*, of Tampa, in 1895, announcing Martí's arrival in Cuban land, and by the newspaper *El Fígaro*, of Havana, on July 26, 1895, communicating the news of the apostle's death."[10]

---

* Date is uncertain.

images. It is important to remember that this teleology began with Martí himself. Ramos argues that Martí dealt with modernity's heterogeneous elements by opposing them to a redemptive teleological project that aspired to raise literature and art as privileged spaces for a possible reconciliation between a utopian past and a dystopian present (Ramos 1989, 145–243). Martí also articulated this project in the visual representations of himself, not only in his writing. Ottmar Ette—in the study of Martí's visual images that has provided a starting point for this book—points out Martí's early interest in constructing an ideal image of himself that could be adapted to the national narrative as he imagined it (Ette 1994, 229–30).

In his 1870 prison portrait (Figure 1.3), we see the 17-year-old Martí posing in chains inside what looks like a room in the jail where he was imprisoned. Martí—or "Prisoner 113" as he was classified—used the back of a copy of this photograph to write a poem to his mother in which he both alludes to his sacrifice for his country and expresses his filial love.

From a critical position, it is important to interrogate the role that Martí himself could have played considering this photo was taken of him in such a terrible place and situation and also ask how he obtained a Doric column on which to rest his left arm in a pose typical of the pictures of that era. Maybe the picture with the column was the way inmates were photographed in that prison. What seems indisputable is that Martí participated actively in the construction of his image, which is precisely what is indicated in the dedications written on the two copies of the photo. In the apostrophe to his mother ("Look at me mother, and for your love for me don't cry; / If, enslaved to my youth and my doctrines, / I filled your martyr's heart with thorns, / Think that among thorns flowers grow"),[12] the young Martí calls for a particular gaze to fall on his photo and appeals to his mother to read it in a certain way: the adolescent enthralled by his duty and his country. The meaning of that gaze, we now know, would later be inculcated in all of us Cubans. Something similar happens in the dedication by Martí to his closest friend Fermín Valdés Domínguez ("Brother-in-pain,

Figure 1.3   Prisoner José Martí (original photograph), 1870

"Photo of Martí in a prisoner's uniform, after being condemned to six years in prison for treason. He dedicated a copy to his mother, Doña Leonor Pérez, writing, '1 Brigade 113' below; and, on the back: *Look at me mother, and for your love for me don't cry; / If, enslaved to my youth and my doctrines, / I filled your martyr's heart with thorns, / Think that among thorns flowers grow./ J. Martí/ Garrison, August 28, 1870.* He sent another copy to Fermín Valdés Domínguez, prisoner in La Cabaña, with the dedication: *Brother-in-pain, never look / at the slave in me who cries like a coward. — / See the robust image of my soul / And the beautiful page of my history./ J. Martí/ Garrison, August 28, 1870.*"[11]

never look / at the slave in me who cries like a coward. — / See the robust image of my soul / And the beautiful page of my history")[13] in which Martí himself organizes and directs the gaze of his friend toward the photo, telling him explicitly *what to see* and *what not to see* in it (Bejel 2009). Nevertheless, it should not seem too strange to us that, despite his youth, Martí was already so aware of his political image, given that a year before he was imprisoned, he had written the dramatic poem "Abdala" (Martí 1869) in which, as Francisco Morán indicates, "all the ethical and patriotic traits that will distinguish [Martí] already appear" (Morán 2007, 345–46). In this dramatic poem (whose classical theme finds inspiration in the teachings of Rafael María de Mendive, Martí's tutor), the protagonist Abdala dies defending his country in his very first encounter with the enemy. It would seem that, interpreted from a nationalistic perspective, Martí, from a very young age, had sketched the personal and political destiny that would culminate in his dramatic death in Dos Ríos on May 19, 1895. All this, of course, is a retrospective interpretation of what happened.

However, regardless of whether we can talk about the appearance of an early heroic project in his 1870 prison photo (with the corresponding dedications to his mother and his friend), one certainly can argue that if Martí's objective in the 1870 photo was to begin to represent himself as a revolutionary hero, his image may present some difficulties: he looks too young and too short (Martí was barely five feet tall), his face is too round and, ironically, appears in a pose reminiscent of the fin-de-siècle style. In other words, this photo presents a Martí looking very different from typical revolutionary leaders like, say Antonio Maceo or Emiliano Zapata. In effect, the transformations undergone by this particular image highlight, from as early as 1895, the possible intention to alter it with the objective to make it more consonant to the image of a heroic figure. Even as Martí went off to war in 1895, someone (we have not yet discovered whom) altered the photograph (Figure 1.4), which appears nothing like the original. In the manipulated photograph,

Figure 1.4   Prisoner José Martí (manipulated photo), date unknown

"It appeared [together with a copy of the photo of Figure 1.2] on a flyer distributed by the newspaper *Cuba*, of Tampa, Florida, in 1895, in order to announce Martí's arrival on Cuban soil, and by the newspaper *El Fígaro*, of Havana, on May 26, 1895, when the news of the Apostle's death was published."[14]

Martí looks taller, with a prominent jawline and, of course, without the column (now his left arm floats absurdly in the air).

Although it may be impossible to prove beyond doubt, this altered photo is likely the most widely disseminated in Cuban popular culture. For example, the only portrait of Martí's incarceration included in the well-known book *Martí revolucionario* (Revolutionary Martí) by Ezequiel Martínez Estrada is the modified version, as is the case with most other Cuban scholarly and popular culture texts. The changes to the jail photo show that whoever authored them obviously thought that Martí's "elegant" pose should be eliminated to better project the image of a manly revolutionary leader, one who would distance itself from such effete postures. The "naturalness" or lack of "pose" is thus added to the discourse of martyrdom seen in the dedications Martí wrote on the original photo for his mother and best friend. This is also a way of distancing Martí from so-called modernist decadence.[15]

The manipulation of this image seems endless; in 2002 a bronze statue (Figure 1.5) was dedicated in Havana.

Supposedly based on the jail photo, the bronze Martí appears with physical characteristics that do not match the original image. Further, the shift from an iconic *photograph* to an iconic *statue* is significant, given the fact that the latter can invoke the living figure by presenting it three-dimensionally in space. Not only is Martí's image now that of a fairly svelte young man, but the column is also gone (now the left arm is placed closer to the body to avoid leaving it in the air as in the manipulated version of the 1870 photo of Figure 1.4) and a pickaxe has been placed in the right hand (although this symbolizes the prisoner's forced labor, there is certainly no pickaxe to be seen in the original photo). Everything directly related to the photo of "Prisoner 113" is part of what Roberto Tejada—using Maurice Merleau-Ponty to analyze twentieth-century Mexican photography—calls the "ambience of the image." Tejada argues that an image is always surrounded by a discursive and experiential ambience that mediates what we see, causing us to see it in a particular way and not in another (Tejada 2009; Merleau-Ponty 1968, 130–41). Additionally, this act of

Figure 1.5 "Prisoner 113," José Martí (bronze statue), by José Ramón Villa Soberón, 2002

"Among the most recent [statues of Martí], Prisoner 113 stands out. It was conceived by José Villa, based on the photo taken of Martí in prison, in 1870. Erected at Martí's Forge, where the remnants of the San Lázaro quarries can still be found, it manifests one of the most striking characteristics of this sculptor: the resignification that occurs upon placing them in real contexts."[16]

contemplating the image simultaneously permits us to "see" the photo as already full of meaning and dims our reflective capacity, making us think that we are seeing the image objectively. We can thus affirm that Martí's poems to his mother and friend, his pose (with or without the column), the discourse of masculinity, the pickaxe, and so many other details create the meaning of what we really "see" when we "look" at Martí's prison image. Only by becoming aware of these and other mediations can we glimpse the possibility of critically understanding what we actually see when looking at Prisoner 113 and of revealing the mechanisms of the image's production and distribution that have conditioned our way of "seeing" it. We can say, therefore, that the historical event is not the cause of what we see when looking at Martí's image, but the effect produced by its retrospective reconstruction according to the political and emotional exigencies of the present knowledge we have acquired about that picture. By being aware of these mechanisms we will be able to resignify Martí and perhaps the nation.

TOTAL AWARENESS

The year 1891 is extremely important for Martí's iconography because by that time he had reached a crucial stage in his preparations for the Cuban War of Independence and he also took part that year in the American International Monetary Comission (AIMC) as the delegate for Uruguay. Martí also published *Versos sencillos* (Martí 1975b, 59–126)[17] and the influential essay "Our America" (Martí 1975a, 6, 15–23; originally published in *La Patria Libre* on January 30, 1891) that same year and had his portrait painted by the Swedish artist Herman Norrman—an oil on canvas done in Martí's residence at 120 Front Street in New York. A year later, in 1892, Martí founded the Cuban Revolutionary Party and was elected as its representative. Additionally during this time, Martí was the victim of biting accusations from some of his countrymen (especially Enrique Collazo, a veteran of the Ten Years' War), who called him *Capitán araña* (Captain

Spider), which meant to accuse him of organizing from exile an unnecessary war in which many Cubans would die and in which Martí himself was not even going to directly participate. Martí was offended and flustered by these accusations, and they seem to have been the cause of a deep depression (López 2006, 38). These and other events and circumstances most likely influenced his subsequent desire to increase the control of his public image, including his visual image (Ette 1994, 251–52). This can help explain why his post-1891 bust portraits are the most iconic ones (Figure 1.6 is a good example). They all display a very serious Martí with an almost visionary gaze: his eyes do not meet the camera's lens but instead look to one side as though intensely contemplating something beyond the camera, his hands are rarely seen, and he appears in a humble suit (this type of dress was considered very modest at the time). All of this creates what we might call an *aesthetic of authenticity and poverty.*

The only exception—an important one—to this aesthetic in Martí's post-1891 bust portraits is found in the photo taken of him in Washington, DC (Figure 1.7), where he appears very well dressed, sitting in an elegant, high-backed chair, with his hands visible in a position designed to effect a thinker's pose.

Gonzalo de Quesada y Miranda writes that his father Gonzalo de Quesada y Aróstegui and the Puerto Rican patriot Sotero Figueroa used to swear that Martí hated this photo because for him the pose seemed "petulant." Martí reportedly blamed the photographer for insisting on the pose (which may very well be true, given what we know about the characteristics of the other photos taken of Martí in those years). In other words, this photo presents an overly elegant Martí in an obviously contrived pose that reduces the effect of naturalness, poverty and humility that he wished to create for his ideal image. Moreover, Martí's protest upon seeing the photo reveals his awareness of his image and his interest in controlling the way it was projected. It should be added that in the same AIMC meeting, Martí drew some tiny self-portraits in the margins of his notebook. The best known of these drawings is perhaps the

Figure 1.6   "José Martí in Jamaica, 1892"

"Picture of Martí taken on October 10, 1892, in Kingston, Jamaica, by the patriot and photographer Juan Bautista Valdés: There is a copy with the following dedication: *To the eminent son of Cuba that defends her from her dangers and honors her with his creative life, to my selfless and virile friend José Mayner, his José Martí, October 13, 1892.* This copy has been impressed in raised letters the photographer's signature and the inscription: *J. B. Valdés—Studio—85 Kenn Street—Kingston.* There is another copy dedicated by Martí to Esteban Borrero: *To his brother Esteban, Pepe. New York.*"[18]

Figure 1.7   "José Martí in Washington, 1891"

"Picture of Martí made in Washington. According to the Puerto Rican patriot Sotero Figueroa, the picture was taken during the days in which the International American Monetary Commission was taking place, and in which Martí represented the Republic of Uruguay. Figueroa and Gonzalo de Quesada y Aróstegui affirmed that Martí was not pleased with this picture because he consider petulant the pose chosen by the photographer."[19]

Figure 1.8 "José Martí's self-portrait, 1891"

"Self-portrait of Martí. The original measures only two centimeters high. In the same sheet of paper there are other drawings by him and the phrase *For America*, repeated several times."[20]

one in Figure 1.8, which has been widely disseminated as part of his iconography.

In addition to revealing details about Martí's intentionality in his graphic self-representation, the drawing in Figure 1.8 shows a funnel- or bulb-shaped head with an exaggerated forehead and brooding eyes, two characteristics that also appear in the most iconic of his images after 1891. It seems Martí's interest in constructing and controlling his image strengthened after that year, to the point that Ottmar Ette wonders whether Martí was his own first censor (Ette 1994, 236). I would add that he was perhaps his own first *manipulator*. But here we must consider that, as Ette himself clarifies, in the latter half of the nineteenth century—the high point of photographic portraiture—the act of capturing a photographic image was much more intense and less automatic than it is in our day, where we see "an avalanche of images" (Ette 1994, 230). Ette continues: "That intensity was doubtless owed to the fact that the subject had a great awareness of self-representation induced by the technical conditions that required longer periods of preparation and illumination, such that 'instant' photos were practically impossible. Thus, the subject would assume the expression of a *photographed* person, rather than his everyday look. For that reason, a pose consciously adopted is susceptible to being 'read' as an intentional act of interpretation or self-interpretation" (Ette 1994, 230).

Another type of photographic images of Martí are the ones in which he appears with his son José Francisco. Perhaps the most interesting one of these is the photo taken in 1879 of Martí with his son, just a few months old, in his arms (Figure 1.9).

This 1879 photo was taken in Havana on a short trip to his homeland during the so-called Peace of Zanjón. Here, Martí's notable relaxation contrasts with his other known photos: although his eyes continue to be the source of the portrait's charm, this time his expression is happy, almost playful, and he is seated on the ground with his son José Francisco. Is this a side of Martí that we are not too aware due to the state's dissemination of manipulated images and even the demands that Martí imposed on himself in

Figure 1.9   José Martí with his son, 1879

"Martí with his son José Francisco. This zincography was probably made in the city of Havana."[21]

some of his other, more well-known portraits? The answer is probably in the affirmative, since this is a photo in which Martí appears to have lowered his guard, failing to maintain his iconic image (with its seriousness and evasive gaze) that often conceals the most human aspects of his personality, the characteristics hidden behind those serious and calculated portraits. The 1879 photo, probably unintentionally on his part, reveals an image of Martí the tender father, and also a humanized and carefree Martí, something that it is not apparent in any of his other pictures. In the 1879 photo, it seems that Martí has suspended his firm determination to project an image that tries at all cost to equate his visual image with a strict vision of his political and ideological objectives. If we take a close and critical look at the images, we can see throughout his photographs the representation of many Martís: the humble man as well as the elegant one, the young martyr as well as the calculating politician, and the worrisome leader as well as the tender and playful father. On one hand there is the consciously staged image of the politician, and on the other a very multifaceted human being.

In conclusion, Martí's portraits reveal a countenance and gaze of the sitter that often salvages a sense of the individual subjectivity that the medium or *studium* attempted to destroy. Martí's insistence in appearing ever more humble and without any type of adornments in his portraits also points to his antibourgeois and anticommercialization position and his conceptualization of art for the sake of political mobilization.[22] In fact, the more we study his most iconic portraits the more they seem closer to the typical daguerreotype images of bourgeois people. In other words, the simplicity sought by Martí, especially his post-1891 photographs, coincides not with the growing commercialized and serialized bourgeois photography of the time where the sitter appeared surrounded by symbols of wealth but with some of the simpler daguerreotype images of people that dominated the world just before the evolution of daguerreotype into photography.[23]

CHAPTER 2

BATTLING FOR THE NATIONAL ICON

MONUMENTS IN JEOPARDY

IN LATIN AMERICA, THE APOGEE OF MONUMENT building in honor of dead national heroes took place between the last years of the nineteenth and the beginning of the twentieth century (Achúgar 2003, 208–9). This is the time when new nation states like Cuba (whose First Republic began in 1902) deepened their ceremonial repertoireas a way for their new governments to acquire legitimacy. Monument building as well served to articulate a sense of national history and memory (Winter 2010, 322; Nora 1989, 7–25). As Hugo Achúgar states about the official Latin American monuments: "the place of the monument, in peripheral countries, is the place of memory and the place from which one speaks, from which authority speaks [. . .] monumentalization of memory proclaimed a single, national, homogenizing memory" (Achúgar 2003, 191; 208–9). Nevertheless, in spite of the official proclamations of national univocity and homogeneity, monuments—Martí's among them—have almost always been sites where opposing discourses of power do battle or negotiate for control of national memory and authority over knowledge itself.[1] Martí's monuments often become sites of countervoices to authority, expressions of discontent, controversy, reappropriation, and opposition. This is why both Cuban national governments and political groups of different persuasions try so hard to affirm Martí's heroic iconicity, acquire control of their respective audiences, and undermine their opponents' histories and memories.

In addition to the ceaseless ideological battles concerning Martí's monuments, the monuments are also surrounded by an ever-present threat of indifference and forgetfulness by the national subjects who are supposed to always remember their martyr-hero in an unconditionally reverent way. As Carlos Monsiváis so insightfully expresses in reference to contemporary Mexico's national territorial markers, monuments to heroes become so familiar that we often pass through the parks where they have been erected, and we hardly realize that they're anything more than a piece of stone (Monsiváis 1995, 122). This threat of amnesia or indifference toward national monuments in Latin America is what Achúgar calls "the specter of a collective Alzheimer's [that] haunts the end of the present [20th] century" (Achúgar 2003, 192). As such, there are two opposing forces that usually accompany Martí's monuments: the struggles among political and civic groups for the appropriation of the legitimacy that those monuments provide and the fear on the part of those same groups that the memory of the martyr-hero might be forgotten by the citizens. From this fear comes the constant effort—usually via rituals, commemorations, and demonstrations—by pressure groups to make sure that this oblivion never happens.

But the problematic of public memory regarding Martí's national monuments—besides official claims to univocity and the corresponding fear of multivocality and forgetfulness of national sites—leads to other fundamental questions: What is the relationship between opposing histories and memories in the battles for the appropriation of Martí's monuments? What are some of the political implications of the construction and commemorations of Martí's monuments intended to be part of the national heritage and of those built outside Cuban national territory? What (dis)connections can be found between the artistic styles of these monuments and the speeches and rituals celebrated around them? As with almost all monuments, Martí lacks the absolute gravitas and univocity implicated in some of the discourses of power that accompany the ritual celebrations that take place around them and the official reasons given for their construction. In fact, the styles, construction, and events associated with some of Martí's most noteworthy monuments reveal enormous contradictions behind the semblance of unity and reverence incited by the political interests that have promoted their construction and/or commemorations. My objective in this chapter is to uncover these contradictions and discuss their possible meanings, taking into consideration that economic and cultural globalization and revolutions in technology and media entail a radical reevaluation of the national past and its representations.

MONUMENTALIZING MARTÍ

The Cuban state's desire to use Martí's image to its own advantage at different moments of the nation's history is evident in the countless monuments to Martí that dot the country, and in the grandiose public rituals of commemoration that accompany the dedication of some of the largest of these monuments to the apostle (Gonçalves 2006, 18–33). From early on in the twentieth century, many of Martí's best-known monuments have been the center of contentious political and ideological struggles even before they were built, and after their construction these monuments have been the stage for all sorts of political rituals and demonstrations in which opposing factions battle to co-opt Martí's image for their own purposes. There is often a disconnect among official inauguration speeches, commemorative rituals, and the political situation of the nation at the moment of the inauguration, as well as between the implications of the artistic style of the monument and some of the political displays around it.

THE CLASSICAL TEACHER: HAVANA'S CENTRAL PARK, 1905

The monumentalization of José Martí started in the early years of Cuba's First Republic (which began in 1902), and it was during this time that the Cuban state began to use Martí's iconography as a way to control political crises (Guerra 2005, 1–2, 113–18, 255–60). At the beginning of Cuba's First Republic, political harmony hung by

Figure 2.1   "Havana's Central Park monument, 1905"

Monument in Havana's Central Park designed by the Cuban sculptor José Villalta Saavedra (1865–1912).[2] The Western classical style of this monument is meant to lend a certain prestige, dignity, and authority to Martí's image and, therefore, to those who tried to identify themselves with it.

Source: The Carol M. Highsmith Archive, Library of Congress, Prints and Photographs Division, 2010

a thread, land was not distributed to veterans of the War of Independence, and protection was not given to Cuban business. Few Cubans during Martí's lifetime knew much about him (Martí was deported to Spain at the age of 17 and lived in New York for the last 15 years of his life), but when Cubans in the United States began to return to their country in 1898, his fame started to grow. The Cuban National Congress only began observing its "solemn sessions" in Martí's honor in 1905, when the first monument (Figure 2.1) was erected. After this date there was a veritable explosion of events and ceremonies to honor Martí. The monument was placed in Havana's Central Park, dedicated to Martí on February 24, 1905, by Cuba's first president, Tomás Estrada Palma (1902–6). Present at the dedication were Estrada Palma and other political, ecclesiastic, and military dignitaries, including General Máximo Gómez, who had survived the War of Independence (Guerra 2005, 153–222). Martí's image in this monument is clearly that of a *teacher* with disciples—women, men, and children—around the base of the monument as if receiving lessons from the knowledgeable pedagogue. In addition to the teaching theme, the palm branches held by some of the people represented at the statue's base suggest that Martí is exhorting them to sacrifice. Contrary to his reputation as a leader who loved kindness and equality, this monument depicts a hero in marble, dictating from on high with the "people" in a position of inferiority. This contrast is due, at least in part, to the hierarchical characteristic of most classical statuary, but it also suggests the hierarchical organization that the Cuban government was trying to affirm for the society at large and that was displayed during the inaugural celebrations (Gonçalves 2006, 19–22). This was also an image of Martí meant to legitimize Estrada Palma's new government, which had in fact distanced itself from any association of Martí as revolutionary, much less as anti-imperialist (Gonçalves 2006, 19–22).

The plan to build the first monument was announced in 1899 but took six years to be erected—not for lack of funds, but rather due to considerable uncertainty about Cuba's political future: four years of American occupation (1898–1902), followed by what many

Cubans considered to be a puppet government (President Tomás Estrada Palma [1902–6]), and the Platt Amendment imposed on the 1901 Constitution, which gave the United States the right to intervene at will in the island's affairs. As Lillian Guerra asks, how could Martí be honored as a symbol of a nation that did not really exist as such? Everything indicates that the more fragmented the country is, the more appeals are made to Martí's image as a way of consolidating the state's power (Guerra 2005, 1–21, 113–18, 255–60). Starting on February 24, 1905, when the first monument to Martí was unveiled, Martí's monumentalization by the Cuban state began to coincide with an era of foreign investment and commercialization in the island.

THE LOST RELIC: SANTIAGO'S MAUSOLEUM, 1951

After the 1905 construction of Havana Central Park monument, the next most architecturally and politically significant of Martí's monuments is the 1951 mausoleum erected in his honor in Santiago de Cuba. This mausoleum—built by the sculptor Mario Santí[3]—was dedicated in Santiago's Santa Ifigenia Cemetery with several speeches, including one by President Carlos Prío Socarrás (1948–52), who, in spite of his government's reputation for corruption, did everything possible to connect Martí's memory and the highest democratic virtues with his own presidency. As João Felipe Gonçalves demonstrates, other ideas that dominated the speeches that day were that of a Martí who loved liberty and who had become a martyr upholding it (Gonçalves 2006, 27–32). Whatever ideals Prío Socarrás may have expounded that day, anything resembling democracy was violated a few months later (March 10, 1952) by General Fulgencio Batista's military coup d'etat (Gonçalves 2006: 22–27). As such, Martí's mausoleum was built under extremely negative political circumstances for the nation, and there is a marked contrast between the ideals expressed in the inauguration-day speeches and the political situation of the nation at that moment.

Besides the political turmoil around the inauguration of the mausoleum, it is important to discuss the issue of the significance of Martí's remains, which were supposedly buried somewhere in the mausoleum. As I explain in detail in Chapter 4, Martí's corpse traveled from the point of Dos Ríos (where he was killed on May 19, 1895) to the first place he was buried in Remanganaguas, and after other stops that lasted a few days, it ended in Santiago de Cuba's Santa Ifigenia Cemetery. The Spanish government buried him in a common grave, and it was not until 1907 that the Cubans transferred his remains to a tomb called the Templete (Gonçalves 2006, 22). In spite of the fact that many Cubans believed that this was not a dignified tomb for the hero of the nation, it took a few decades (into the early 1940s) until some members of Santiago's Rotary Club managed to raise funds and gain support from the public and the government to start building a grandiose tomb to bury Martí's remains. It was during the presidency of Ramón Grau San Martín (1944–48) that a competition was established for a new mausoleum. By 1947 the winning project was selected, but the construction was so slow that the project was not finished until 1951 during President Carlos Prío Socarrás administration. Prío Socarrás appointed as Minister of Public Works Santiago's mayor Luis Casero, who accelerated the construction of Martí's "final" tomb and unveiled the mausoleum on June 30, 1951 (Gonçalves 2006, 23).

The inaugural celebration was tumultuous, and as Gonçalves states, "[l]ike the dedication of the statue at the Parque Central [1905], Martí's 1951 funeral was a great ritual of reinforcement of hierarchies. [. . .] the separation of social categories was publicly performed and therefore legitimized" (2006, 24). But, besides the politics surrounding the mausoleum, Martí's remains were described by President Prío Socarrás in his speech as "sacred ashes of the apostle" (*Diario de la Marina*, July 1, 1951). In the 1951 mausoleum and in the rituals celebrated around it, there was the tacit implication that Martí's remains were the indexical source that gave physical gravitas to the apostle's heroic and quasi-religious memory and to the significance of the mausoleum itself. In other words, if—according to the terminology of Charles Sanders Peirce[4]— one of the definitions of an *index* is that of a sign pointing to the cause of an effect (like smoke indicates that there is fire somewhere, that that fire is the cause or source of the smoke), Martí's remains can be viewed as the indexical source that gives physical foundation to the significance of Santiago's mausoleum as such. If one of the indexical foundations of the mausoleum is that the remains, the "ashes," of the deceased person are buried somewhere in the site, the following story undermines that assumption.

In 1995, Professor Enrico Mario Santí—son of Mario Santí, the sculptor who helped build José Martí's mausoleum—recounts that his father once told him a terrible secret about the mausoleum (Santí 1995).[5] The sculptor Santí and his assistant were trying to move the coffin in which Martí's remains had been laid to rest from the old tomb to the new mausoleum. After some maneuvers with the crane, Mario Santí "noticed that water was leaking from one of the corners, and that it came from a wide and moldy hole [. . .] My father [professor Santí continues saying] began examining it [the tomb], [and] concluded that neither the crane's hook nor poor instructions could have caused the damage [. . .] To their amazement, however, they discovered something more surprising still: that there was nothing inside. Martí's coffin was empty" (Santí 1995, 71–72). If this account is true, there is nothing left of Martí's physical remains, the relics are completely gone. This is significant to the meaning of the mausoleum, because the existence of the remains is a major part of what a mausoleum is all about, its fundamental meaning.

In the same English version of his essay, Professor Santí states that the original Spanish version of his story had been published in Miami's *Diario de las Américas* on May 20, 1995 (Santí 1995), and that he received several extremely positive responses from other Cubans who had read the essay. Nevertheless, a few weeks later there were two rather negative essays published in the same journal. The later of the two was authored by Luis Casero (the former mayor of Santiago who in 1951 had been appointed by President Prío Socarrás to oversee the construction of the mausoleum), who labeled Santí's account about Martí's remains a "strange assertion" and a "lie" (Casero 1995). Santí defended himself against these attacks, affirming the truthfulness of his account. But what it is interesting to me for the purpose of the present work is not how accurate is Santí's account versus his detractors' (after all, as I said in the introduction of this book, my approach is not historical but closer to a critical retrospective reconstruction of a collective memory about Martí) but how eschatological and even morbid this whole story is. As Santí mentions, some of the readers of his *Diario de las Américas* essay reacted with tears and extreme emotions. Santí himself says that "[t]he reader [of his essay in Spanish] that impressed me the most was a certain colleague, recently arrived from Cuba, who wrote telling me she would keep the essay so that when her daughter grew up she could read it as an example of how Martí should be thought of" (Santí 1995, 75–76). What Santí says is quite significant because it claims that Martí's remains have physically disappeared; there are no possible bodily relics left. I argue that the disappearance narrated in Santí's account means that Martí's remains can no longer function as the indexical foundations of the mausoleum, but instead become an absence that only an act of collective imagination can replace with a holistic meaning that overlooks such a void. In the final analysis, Santí's controversial story about Martí's "ashes" may serve as a deconstructive metaphor of the claim that Martí's remains are *relics* that indicate that something physical (a fetish?) had remained of Martí's real body.

Regarding Martí's relics, we have to direct our attention to what is called the Fragua Martiana (Martí's Forge) in Centro Havana County, in the intersection of the streets Hospital and Vapor (main entrance in the corner of Príncipe and Hospital streets). As Jonathan Dettman suggests, the Fragua Martiana is more than a small museum honoring Martí, it is also a memorial, a place for official studies and activities, and a sort of holy shrine where there are some of Martí's relics in the form of pieces of his clothes, some photographs, soil from where he was killed, and other types of artifacts that are meant to treat Martí's memory with an extreme religious-like reverence.[6] Pictures are forbidden in this museum/shrine, and visitors of all kinds are carefully watched by the museum guardians. The holiness of the site goes back to its foundation. Its history began in 1938 when Gonzalo de Quesada y Miranda (son of Martí's close friend and testamentary executor Gonzalo de Quesada y Aróstegui) and other *martianos* began to investigate the location of the Canteras de San Lázaro (San Lázaro's Shafts) where Martí was imprisoned in 1870 and forced to work in the mines. The site of the Fragua was inaugurated on April 10, 1944, with the presence of President Fulgencio Batista, and in 1946, Carlos Prío Socarrás (at that time Minister of Public Works for President Grau San Martín) showed great interest in the project and promised to Quesada y Miranda that the Fragua would be built ("La Fragua Martiana" n.d.). On January 28, 1952, less than two months before Prío Socarrás presidency would be deposed by Batista's military coup, the news was given in the press that, under the direction of the engineer Manuel Febles Valdés, the Fragua was finally inaugurated. This history is important not only to show that the Fragua is yet another of Martí's sites mired with local politics but also because it highlights the issue of Martí's relics. The Fragua— with the pieces of clothes, the soil from Dos Ríos, and the whole ambience of the museum, memorial, or shrine—is the most shrine-like of Martí's official sites in Havana and probably in the entire nation. Here, more even than in Santiago's mausoleum, there is a feeling of a place built and maintained as a religious sacred site.

FROM NEUTRAL THINKER TO COMBATIVE REVOLUTIONARY: FROM THE CIVIC PLAZA (1958) TO THE REVOLUTION PLAZA (1959–)

As in many of the other monuments honoring Martí, the one in Figure 2.2 was the site of political battles since its inception. But this monument is artistically and politically significant for at least three reasons: the conceptual and artistic implications of the obelisk and the statue; the style choice process for the two sections of the monument; and the dramatic reversal of fortune from December 1958—when the site was about to be finished and become Batista's greatest appropriation of Martí's image—to January 1959, when Fidel Castro (1959–2008) began to reappropriate it. From

Figure 2.2   "Dual Monument in Revolution Plaza, 1958"

Dual Monument: Martí's statue was designed by sculptor Juan José Sicre and architect Aquiles Maza[7] and the obelisk was designed by architect Enrique Luis Varela, President Batista's Minister of Public Works.[8] In December 1958, Fulgencio Batista's government had almost finished building the enormous and stylistically dual Martí's monument in what was then Havana's Civic Plaza when his regime came suddenly to an end and Fidel Castro came to power in January 1959.

Source: The Carol M. Highsmith Archive, Library of Congress, Prints and Photographs Division, 2010

this monument, Castro has delivered some of his most memorable fiery speeches and has gathered the largest popular demonstrations of his regime. In my opinion, this change in the signification of the monument affirms Jay Winter's idea that "alternative interpretation of the political meaning of sites of memory emphasizes the multivocal character of remembrance and the potential for new groups with new causes to appropriate older sites of memory" (2010, 317).

The center of the monument consists of two unequal parts that are conceptually and stylistically unrelated: the enormous obelisk (109 meters) and the comparatively small statue (18 meters) representing a seated Martí reminiscent of Auguste Rodin's famous *The Thinker*. In different ways, both of the artistic styles of the two sections of the monument project a neutralized Martí (perhaps more the obelisk than the statue) bereft of any sense of revolutionary historical context (Gonçalves 2006, 27–32). Moreover, when looking at this site and its surroundings it is difficult to resist the impression of a grandiose fascist monument.[9] It should be noticed that the initial plan for the monument was promoted by Batista himself, who early on in his military career associated himself with Martí's memory in the name of political ambition. The beginning of the monument-building project can be traced to 1938, and the winning prize was awarded in 1943 (during Batista's first presidency) to sculptor Juan José Sicre and architect Aquiles Maza. But the story about how the site ended up with a dual monument of two different styles is rather complicated. Suffice it to say here that although the original project committee chose the Sicre-Maza bid of the statue of Martí seated like Rodin's *Thinker*, Batista's final preference was another complex design in which a statue of Martí was going to appear like a Godlike symbol on top of a tall tower. Batista's choice reflected less his artistic preferences than his close friendship with Minister of Public Works Enrique Luis Varela. A large public scandal followed Batista's decision, and after a series of political maneuvers and compromises, the president and his government ordered the building of an enormous obelisk next to the statue.[10]

In the history of monument building, there have been many types of monuments, including the sacred sites typical of the Christian Middle Ages and the more contemporary secular ones—the walls that are filled with fallen warriors' names and sites giving the impression of empty spaces, which imply that the extreme violence that is memorialized is such that historical meaning has been lost.[11] The obelisk is usually associated with a secular style that became more common after Protestant countries and groups protested against some Catholic symbols dominating national monuments.[12] Needless to say, Cuba was not (and is not) a Protestant country, but these histories add to the possible meanings of the styles of Martí's monument: the secularity and neutrality of the obelisk and even, to a certain degree, of the statue seems more the effects of political battles than of artistic considerations.

Regardless of Batista's stylistic decision, what it is more dramatic and historically significant about Martí's monument in what it used to be Havana's Civic Plaza—rechristened Revolution Plaza by Castro—is how Castro turned the symbolism of the monument into his most effective political weapon. Despite the "neutralized" stylistic implications of both the obelisk and the statue, Castro managed to identify his revolutionary and anti-imperialist stance with those objects by giving his speeches and organizing massive demonstrations at the base and around the monument. In fact, for several decades after January 1959, Castro's revolution was internationally associated with some of the images of Castro in front of Martí's statue, giving fiery speeches to enormous masses of people. This was a case of reappropriation and not of building a new monument, of renaming the site from Civic Plaza to Revolution Plaza, and of radically changing the meaning of the monument through rituals and massive public demonstrations. The monument has been so politically effective for Castro that it was not until 1996 that his government unveiled its own José Martí Memorial on the base of the monument of the Revolution Plaza. The rituals and demonstrations around the original monument have had enough resignifying power to change its original meaning, regardless its style and previous history.

Figure 2.3   "José Martí's statue in New York's Central Park, 1965"

Equestrian statue of José Martí on Central Park South and Avenue of the
Americas, 1965. Built and donated in 1958 by the American sculptor Anna Hyatt
Huntington,[13] and erected on May 19, 1965, after innumerable political struggles
between Cuban groups and American authorities. The marble pedestal is 19 feet
tall, the bronze Martí on horseback is 18 feet tall, and the whole ensemble is 37
feet tall and weighs 6 tons.

Source: Scott Sendrow (http://www.bridgeandtunnelclub.com), 2012

THE FALLEN WARRIOR: NEW YORK'S
CENTRAL PARK, 1965

As we have seen, Cuban territory has been the site of political disputes over several of Martí's statues and monuments. However, the United States has also seen similar struggles over his image. Perhaps the most representative of these struggles has focused on the equestrian statue of José Martí at New York's Central Park South and the Avenue of the Americas. The struggle involved both pro- and anti-Castro groups, the mayor of New York, the police, New York Parks and Recreation, and even the US State Department.

Although there are countless statues and monuments to Martí in Miami,[14] Tampa, and other cities in Florida, New Jersey, and other US states, the one in New York's Central Park is significant for several reasons: its centrality, conspicuousness, and enormous size; the fact that its dedication was delayed by political battles related to Castro's Revolution (it was completed in 1958 but was not installed until May 1965); and, finally, it is stylistic divergence from other monumental Martí statues in depicting him as an equestrian fallen warrior. Despite the fact that this monument was donated by a US sculptor and installed in New York's Central Park, Cuban authorities were monetarily involved in its construction. It has been reported that in 1957 the Batista government donated $100,000 to the New York Parks and Recreation, supposedly to cover the costs of the marble pedestal (Talese 1964). The statue's total cost at the time was calculated to be $175,000–$200,000 (Talese 1964). Cuban taxpayers contributed, at least partially, to the building of this monument. But the most salient political aspect of the construction of this monument has to be the battles that ensued around it.

Several *New York Times* articles published between 1960 and 1965 about Martí's equestrian statue show how a monument to a Cuban hero can unleash political battles that cross national borders and involve high-level members of the Cuban and US governments.[15] A January 29, 1960, article titled "Central Park Ceremony for Cuban Hero Erupts into Riots over Castro" relates how during a turbulent half hour on January 28 (Martí's birthday), Castro's supporters fought their detractors for "the right to honor the birth-day of José Martí" (*New York Times* 1960). The battleground had been established some weeks in advance when some members of the pro-Castro Movimiento 26 de julio (The 26th of July Move-ment) were told by New York authorities that they had been denied a permit for Martí's birthday celebration at the marble pedestal (at that time only the pedestal had been installed). The article explains that they were not given permission because the bronze statue had not yet been put in place. Nevertheless, Movimiento 26 de julio members soon discovered that an anti-Castro organization called La Rosa Blanca (The White Rose; the white rose is a symbol taken from Martí's *Versos sencillos*) had obtained a permit and planned to place a bouquet of white roses at the foot of the pedestal. On Janu-ary 28 there was a violent encounter around the pedestal between the two groups, and in the end, 3 people were injured and 12 were arrested (6 from each side) before the police riot squads could disperse the crowd (*New York Times* 1960). Castro supporters insulted their opponents as "assassins, murderers," while the anti-Castro group mocked them as "communists, godless blackguards" (*New York Times* 1960). The article reveals not only who the com-batant groups were and what they considered detestable in their opponents but also the extremely aggressive nature of that day's public disturbance. Few of the claims that Martí's image was an inspiration for unity were visible in that encounter.

In 1964, the statue in Central Park still had not been erected. Another *Times* article from October 10, 1964, titled "Cubans Fail in Attempt to Place Martí Statue" describes the crux of the dilemma that emerged that day (Talese 1964, 3). The article explains the origin of the statue and refers to a group of Cuban exiles who had built a plaster copy of the statue to place on the vacant ped-estal. As it turned out, after a midnight escapade involving the use of an enormous truck to transport the giant plaster statue, the Cubans were unable to lift it into place, despite it weighing much less than the original bronze statue. They were forced to return the statue to a nearby place belonging to one of their members. The article describes a series of failures that show the frustration of the participants as well as the unusual entanglements related to this event. But the odyssey-like path of the New York authorities in finally raising the enormous bronze statue is no less absurd. In 1960 it was discovered that, on the advice of the State Department, the statue had been hidden in a Bronx warehouse and placed under constant guard (Talese 1964). The intent was to avoid disturbances and the possibility that pro-Castro groups would occupy the site in order to display their devotion to Martí. In early 1965, the statue was brought from a workshop in Redding, Connecticut, to New York. On January 27, the statue was raised, but it remained covered for a few months. Finally, on May 19, 1965, the *New York Times* published a report saying, "The José Martí statue, that has been the center of pro-Castro controversy, was quietly unveiled at a simple ceremony yesterday morning" (1965c). Sculptor Anna Hyatt Huntington took part in the ceremony. The *New York Times* article includes an ironic coda: "As the dedication ended a broad-shouldered Cuban—tie askew and in need of a shave—quietly placed a single white rose at the base of the pedestal and swiftly left. He wouldn't give his name" (1965c). But on May 26 of that year, the newspaper published a "Letter to the Editor," which stated the following:

> Thank you for publicizing in the news article appearing May 19, the long-delayed unveiling of Anna Hyatt Huntington's fine statue of José Martí, Cuba's great liberator-author. The Cuban who placed the rose at the base of the statue may not have given his name, but the symbolism of his act is immediately apparent to all who know Martí's writings. "I grow a white rose" for friend and foe is the leitmotif of one of his most famous poems, and the sentiment undoubtedly expresses the Cuban martyr's hope for a Western Hemisphere characterized by peace, goodwill and understanding among its peoples. (Mead Jr. 1965, 46)

The international controversy caused by the ideological differences among martianos contrasts with the obvious desire of Robert G. Mead Jr.'s letter to the editor appealing to unity in the face of divided opinion.

Figure 2.4   Anti-Imperialist Tribune statue, 2000

The statue often referred to as "Martí Antiimperialista" (Anti-imperialist Martí) was sculpted by Andrés González González in 2000.[16] The statue appears as the main piece of the Anti-Imperialist Tribune, a colossal park in front of the US Interests Office in Havana (a US building that functions as an "embassy," given the lack of official diplomatic relations between Cuba and the United States). The park and Martí's statue were built as Castro's answer to the international controversy called "Elián González's Affair."

Source: The Carol M. Highsmith Archive, Library of Congress, Prints and Photographs Division, 2010

All these political battles reaffirm the idea that a statue is not just a statue but a site of controversy and dissent, in spite of the fact that the unity discourse returns over and over again to claim that the memory of Martí is or should be that of unity among all factions. As usual in the case of Martí's monument building, there is a disconnect between the claim of unity and the political and civic discord even when the monument, like in this case, is built in another country.

THE BELLIGERENT FATHER: HAVANA'S ANTI-IMPERIALIST TRIBUNE, 2000

Once again, a visual image of Martí is used for political purposes in the battle between political positions and ideologies. The so-called Elián González's Affair (2000) refers to a custody fight over a seven-year-old Cuban boy between Elián's father (backed by the Cuban government) and Elián's Miami relatives (backed by the Cuban-American community in Miami and some US officials). In 1999, Elián's mother had left Cuba for the United States in a small boat with her boyfriend and Elián. During the voyage, Elián's mother drowned. The boy survived and was initially placed by the US government with paternal relatives in Miami, who sought to keep Elián in the United States against his father's wishes that the boy be returned to Cuba. After numerous legal struggles involving family, governments, and international juridical statutes, a US federal judge awarded custody to Elián's father. In June 2000, US authorities took the boy from his relatives at gunpoint and returned him to Cuba. Fidel Castro himself actively participated in this international political struggle and ordered the construction of the Martí statue in a section in Havana christened the Anti-Imperialist Tribune. This example shows how the construction of monuments and other memory sites are often not alternatives to but the direct expression of politics.[17]

Besides the purely political, there is what we could call the purely stylistic description of each of the statues mentioned in this chapter. As I have discussed in the previous sections of this chapter, the 1905 Havana Central Park Martí statue can be described as the "The Classical Teacher," the 1958 Civic Plaza (later Revolution Plaza) statue as "The Neutralized Thinker," and the 1965 New York Central Park statue as "The Fallen Warrior." Following this schema, the representation of Martí built in 2000 in the Anti-Imperialist Tribune can be described as "The Belligerent Father." This sculpture combines several ideological and stylistic aspects that are quite remarkable. From the political perspective, this image of an anti-imperialist Martí has been a constant argument of Castro's regime since its inception, and this claim has been most often expressed in the Cuban media, literary and essay notes, and articles published by Castro's supporters.[18] This image of an anti-imperialist Martí is prominently expressed in the bronze statue that, due to the Elián González Affair, has become internationally recognizable. From the stylistic point of view, the Martí that appears in Figure 2.4 is neither a teacher nor a thinker nor a fallen warrior but rather a muscular and energetic father calling for the protection of the "Son of Cuba" from the invading US enemy. Needless to say, a *muscular* Martí is very far from any knowledge we have of the Martí in his photographs, but what is also remarkable about this statue is the association between Martí's memory and protective fatherhood. Among the most popular photographic images of Martí are those where he appears with his small son in his arms (see an example in Figure 1.9). The fact that in the statue of Figure 2.4 Martí is represented as an aggressive and protective father, as well as a very muscular man and an anti-imperialist figure, provides very powerful characteristics to this image. As Winter states, politics when combined with family images becomes much more effective (2010, 314). In other words, since many political discourses are constructed and reaffirmed by the use of family metaphors and images, representing Martí not only as an aggressive political leader but also as a protective father of the "Son of Cuba" makes the symbolism of the statue much more politically effective.

CONCLUSION

As I have discussed in this chapter, governments—as different as those of Estrada Palma, Prío Socarrás, Batista, and Castro—have appropriated and manipulated the symbolism of Martí's monuments and statues in order to legitimize themselves and centralize state power. Regarding the United States, we have to remember that for several decades since the Castro Revolution, the US government and other American organizations have financed institutions in American territory like "Radio Martí" and "TV Martí" that promote a version of Martí that is supposed to counter Castro's version. But referring especifically to monuments, we can say that monumentalizing Martí—as with most heroic memorializations—is almost always an attempt to fix him in a public space (e.g., a plaza or a park) that can double as a site for patriotic rituals and for propagandizing by the state or pressure groups. The official use of the monuments raised in his memory imply the desire to establish a univocal heroic idea that favors the discourses of power claiming legitimacy through his memory, but critical analysis reveals that the construction and commemorations of Martí's monuments, rather than embodying political and ideological unity and univocity, are largely a scattering of meaning and a struggle among discourses of power. As such, the monument is a privileged site to express these struggles.

I also argue here that although social and political crises have increased official interest in amplifying Martí's prestige and reputation as a form of political control, it is also true that the combination of factors that now allow Martí's iconicity to be questioned—which for much of the twentieth century seem inconceivable—point to the weakening of modernity's great totalizing narratives (including nationalism) and the economic and cultural globalization that promote the rise of new technologies and media. These new historical circumstances—with their ontological implications—make it more obvious than ever that monuments are more than neutral material. They always point to a world of meanings that transcend themselves; they are always simultaneously matter and image.

This is why the rituals of commemoration celebrated around Martí's monuments make a desperate and always ultimately futile attempt to contain discordant meanings. The explicit intention of the monument construction and the discourses and celebrations, the marches and parades, and the written and spoken expressions about the monument in question all try to stop the unstoppable, that which eludes the specific narrative being imposed on them at a given moment by a given group. What emerges from these histories and memories in mutual competition is a series of semantic battlefields, which themselves struggle to avoid the great threat of oblivion or indifference. The instability of meaning in Martí's monuments—and all monuments for that matter—is precisely what permits us to find their critical points, their weaknesses and contradictions, and it is perhaps here where their true interest, their signifying energy, resides. Finally, what is really special regarding Martí's iconography in general and monuments in his honor in particular is that they hardly seem to give signs of change or variation concerning the heroic and almost saintly status of Martí's memorialization. Perhaps, this is only happening in some Cuban works during the so-called Special Period (1990–present)—this is one of the themes of Chapter 4.

CHAPTER 3

THE FILMING OF A MEMORY

Yo pienso, cuando me alegro
Como un escolar sencillo,
En el canario amarillo,—
Que tiene el ojo tan negro!

(When I am happy, I think
like a simple schoolboy,
about the yellow canary
whose eye is so black.)[1]

—José Martí, *Versos sencillos*, 1891

A PERSONAL EXPERIENCE

I HAD THE GOOD FORTUNE TO ATTEND the Charles Chaplin Theater in Havana on December 12, 2010, and to personally experience the extraordinary reaction of the audience to the film *José Martí: El ojo del canario* (*José Martí: The Eye of the Canary* 2010). At a certain moment of the film, all the moviegoers (including myself; after all, I am not immune to Martí's mythification) were crying almost uncontrollably. Once the movie was over, the entire audience, while still crying, gave a standing ovation to the film and several embraced one another. Later I spoke with other Cuban friends who told me, without exception, that they had reacted in the same way when they went to watch the movie.

A Critical Approach

This film has become a major cultural event in Cuba and beyond, and its popular and critical success lies, at least partially, in the fact that it represents a very human Martí. But needless to say, our reaction to the movie has a lot to do with the long history of emotional and ideological teaching about Martí that we Cubans have undergone since our births and to a series of psychological and even historical complexities that all converge in our mind in the moment we watch the movie. These audience reactions to *José Martí: The Eye of the Canary* crystalize several themes central to the function of Martí's visual image in contemporary Cuba. But the film's reception by people influenced by the Cuban national narrative raises key questions, including the following: Why does today's observer (familiar with Martí's life and work) react to the film with such emotion? How does the film contribute to reactivating our reaction to Martí's photographic and pictorial icons? What do these moving images of Martí—contextualized by the film's overall historical and familial ambientation—add to our visual repertoire of our long-gone martyr-hero?

My claim is that what an interested observer—influenced by the Cuban national narrative—experiences when watching this film (especially on the big screen) is, probably, a series of instantaneous memory associations between still photographic images and moving film ones. I also argue that in this film, even the historical and familial contextualizations and the moments in which Martí is represented in a very human manner, serve to increase the purely emotional and ideological mythification of Martí instead of promoting his possible resignification. By deconstructing these emotional reactions—ideologically formed by the teaching of the Cuban national narrative—I hope to provide an anti-ideological critique of the affective response to the film.

A RECIPROCAL GAZE BETWEEN
OBSERVER AND OBSERVED

There is no doubt that an analysis of the Martí character's gaze is unavoidable when discussing this film. The director of the movie, Fernando Pérez himself—in email correspondence with me—stated, "In the GAZE [emphasis in the original] of the child and the adolescent I sought a GAZE [emphasis in the original] that would reflect the observers sensibility, that is, the gaze of a budding poet (as a child) that begins to flower (as an adolescent)" (Director Fernando Pérez, pers. comm., January 13, 2011). In other words, Pérez wants to make sure that the two actors representing Martí are able to establish an emotional connection with the viewer. The actor Daniel Romero, who plays the teenage Martí, spoke in an interview about his experience with the director: "[Fernando] put me through an exchange of glances test, a theater exercise that consisted in visually transmitting different emotions to him [. . .]. When he looked at me then, teary-eyed, I knew that he had given me some personal experience of his own" (Daumont 2011). Given this information by the director and one of the main actors, it seems imperative that to begin to critically approach this work we must take into consideration our memory of Martí's previous visual images (especially, but not exclusively, some of his photographs) and their relation to the national hero's representation in the film.

As I argued in previous chapters, two basic ideas are central to understanding the ways that Martí's visual image functions: the *retrospective reconstruction* that the interested observer undertakes of what he or she sees, and the process of the *reciprocal gaze* between the observer and the subject of the image—moving in the case of film, static in the case of photography.[2] Additionally, the use of Martí's photographic images as index of the real Martí, as well as symbol for Cuba, shapes the ways the film functions in our contemporary memory. What I am arguing here is, on the one hand, that the filmic representations of Martí convey, to some extent, the indexical implication of the photographic images that are the bases of the nondigital film, and to this we have to add the symbolic implications of our memory of a hero who is supposed to represent the whole nation. In conclusion, the indexical effect (with the implications of the existence of a real referent) and the symbolic effect (in this case Martí as symbol of the Cuban nation) support each other in the memory experience of the interested observer who watches the film.[3]

Regarding the resemblance (or lack of it) between the photographic images of Martí and his filmic representations played by Damián Rodríguez (child Martí) and Daniel Romero (older Martí), Director Pérez tells me that his cast of the child Martí was inspired by the photograph taken of the boy at age nine, which, as mentioned previously, is the earliest existing image of the national hero (see Figure 1.1).[4] Consequently, the fact that the film represents Martí from nine years onward has much to do with the boy's age in his first known photograph. This directorial choice highlights one of the photographic bases of nondigital film: the indexicality of the photographic image implies that at certain moment a real Martí was in front of the camera that took the picture. This is an important aspect of the effect and affect of the possible memory association between Martí's first photo and the film character representing the child Martí even when the physical similarities are far from exact. But although there are no strong resemblances between the photographic image of Martí's 1862 photo and its representation on the screen, I argue that the sad eyes of both the photo and the film images, as well as the age of the movie character and the entire "ambientation" of the film, seem to be sufficient for an interested observer to *emotionally* connect the movie character with the real referent Martí.

As I elaborate in this book's first chapter, the 1862 photograph shows Martí as a child in the Havana Mestre's gallery. As present-day observers, when looking at this image, we may ask ourselves, "What might this child, who would later become such an important figure in Cuban and Latin American history, be thinking and feeling at that moment?" This curiosity is one of the aspects that the film tries to satisfy by placing that child in a familial, social, and historical context, represented by color, sound, and movement.

Figure 3.1   Film still representing José Martí the child, 2010

Film still from *José Martí: The Eye of the Canary*. Martí the child (played by Damián Rodríguez) shows his fearful eye in one of the many moments when his father is expressing his anger about something related to either financial problems or injustices that he perceives at the workplace. In the film, there is an emphasis on representing Martí the child with very sad eyes. This is an aspect that coincides with a characteristic of Martí's first photo, which we have studied in the first chapter. But other than the sad eyes and the approximate age, we must call our attention to the fact that there is little physical similarity between the images of Martí's first photo and the character of child Martí in the film.

This probably explains why much of the film evokes such intense reactions from those of us familiar with Martí's life and work. A photograph like the one from 1862—which itself contains indexical traces of the past (a contiguity with a concrete historical place and time)—arrives in the present already bearing all those discourses that have made Martí a national, even hemispheric, figure. It is within this dynamic that we see Martí's image represented on screen.

But it should be made clear that the director has stated that his intention was never to make the film images of Martí (compare Figure 3.1 and Figure 1.1) an exact copy of his existing photographic portraits: "I didn't propose to find an exact physical resemblance because there is no single reference for the child and adolescent Martí. The predominant image for most Cubans is the adult Martí (which proliferates at times on busts and deformed statues)" (Director Fernando Pérez, pers. comm., January 13, 2011). This explains, in part, the fact that Fernando Pérez's representation of the 17-year-old Martí was inspired by an 1872 portrait where Martí was actually 19 years old (compare Figure 3.2 and Figure 3.3). When I asked him if I was correct in my impressions about the visual inspiration behind the casting of the actor who represents the 17-year-old Martí in the movie, Pérez told me, "Your observations about the reference images are EXACT [emphasis in the original] [. . .] The adolescent Martí is inspired by the Madrid photo" (see Figure 3.2; Director Fernando Pérez, pers. comm., January 13, 2011).[5] What can be gathered from all these declarations and from the comparisons between some of Martí's photos and the images of the two characters (Martí the child and Martí the adolescent played by Daniel Romero) in the movie is that, on the one hand, the film plays with the incomplete memory that the interested observer probably has of the preadult photographic images of Martí; and, on the other, there is a creation of cinematographic images of the martyr-hero that—although makes our memory react retrospectively when we watch the film—are not identical to those of the photographs of Martí at the age in question. What is happening here, according to Pérez, is a general memory incompleteness on the part of the interested observer, who probably does not have a very clear visual image of the Martí of those years; in other words, there is less awareness on the part of the interested observer of how Martí actually did look on his photographic images of his childhood and adolescence. But in the final analysis, this interested observer, the faithful one, is more than willing to overlook image differences and be overtaken by the general message and ambientation of the work. It is a matter of illusion and allusion: the disposition of these moviegoers is to accept that what they are watching is just an illusion of reality on the one hand and to willingly be overtaken by emotion with the visual allusion of what they are watching on the other.

The discussion of the iconic resemblance and symbolism between photograph images of Martí and their representations in the film, brings us to Andrea Noble's suggestive proposal, based on one of Roland Barthes's key principles in *Camera Lucida*, that the study of Latin American national heroes' images must start with the idea that the photographic image—although it appears as an objective historical fact (Charles Sanders Peirce's concept of the *index* sign also points to a real referent) or an act of recovering for memory something absent in the moment of observation—also produces a simultaneous act of "counter-memory" because its visual impact seems to assure us that the image is simply "there" and that there is no need to contextualize it (Noble 2005; Barthes 1980). Although *José Martí: The Eye of the Canary* supplies a familial and historical context to the images in question, this contextualizing feature of this particular film, instead of demystifying the memory, serves to reactivate and even increase the audience's patriotic and personal feelings about José Martí. Therefore, it should remain clear that the movie actually heightens rather than diminishes Martí's mythic quality by emphasizing images that serve to increase our empathy for the main character. The historical process that contextualizes the cinematographic Martí ends up more closely related to mystifying retrospective memory than to a properly historical recreation because it leaves little room for a critical view of Martí—that is, the iconographic transformation of certain images in the film works as a retrospective reactivation of some of the effects associated with

Figure 3.2   José Martí's face from a Madrid photo, 1872

Detail of Martí's face from an 1872 photograph taken in Madrid in which he appears
with Fermín and Eusebio Valdés Domínguez. At the time of the shot, Martí was 19
years old. As it is easy to ascertain, there are more physical similarities in this image
compared with Figure 3.3 than Martí's 1862 photo compared with Figure 3.1.

Figure 3.3   Film still representing the adolescent José Martí, 2010

Film still of the actor Daniel Romero playing a 17-year-old Martí. This still image of
Romero shows perhaps the closest similarity to the 1872 photograph of Martí.

previous Martí's images.[6] More than a historical critique, what determines the way in which the interested viewer observes and reads these images is nothing other than the emotional and ideological baggage conditioned by the many discourses of power that have contributed to creating the sense of belonging to and representing the nation as an "imagined community" (Anderson 1983).

Another aspect of the film's emotional effectiveness refers to a tropologically complex process that pertains both to Martí's photographs and pictorial images and to his filmic ones. These images function simultaneously as a synecdoche and as a symbol: an image of a specific person (Martí in this case as an indexical referent) representing a complicated and heterogeneous historical phenomenon like the Cuban nation itself. Therefore, Martí's film image, like his photos and other pictorial images, functions as a part and a metaphor of the national whole, which points us toward the desire of imagining the nation as a homogeneous unity encapsulated in the images of a single martyr-hero. It is not difficult to assert, thus, that this tropological process, due to its complexity and unconscious signification, helps to produce the emotional impact of Martí's film image.

When looking at one of Martí's images, whether static in a photograph or in motion on the big screen (there are, of course, important visual and philosophical differences if we watch the movie on a big screen, a television, a laptop, or an iPhone because size affects our reaction to what we look at), we participate in two simultaneous moments: the *past* of that image that moves us (contextualized in various ways in the film) and the *present* from which we observe (conditioned by the legitimizing discourses of the nation and by our own personal experience in relation to Martí's image). In other words, the process we experience when we watch these images is not only reciprocal between observer and observed, but it also forces us to participate in an ideological and emotional effect in the present, especially if we have been influenced by the Cuban national narrative. I believe that a critical analysis of Martí's images allows us to become conscious of the mediation that exists in the act of looking at Martí's bodily image.

All this means that looking at Martí's cinematographic image may produce a complex and paradoxical effect in viewers, one that implies a spatial and temporal distance, but that simultaneously creates an emotional effect that invites us not only to erase that distance but also to momentarily suspend the knowledge that we are really only looking at a filmic representation (what in film studies is called "affective suspension of disbelief") of a historical figure. Also, as I said before, what perhaps seduces us the most regarding the 1862 photo is the boy Martí's sad, startled look, which seems to distance him from the normativity of that era's photography-studio conventions, since we perceive the background of that studio (with all its pressures and poses) counterposed against the surprised child. Similarly, the filmic version of the young boy represents him as one who scarcely speaks and almost always faces his surroundings—the father's tirades, the mother's affections, the colonial world's turbulence and abuses, the slaves' suffering, and so on—with that same sad gaze. Regardless of the lack of exact visual similarities, for the observer who knows something about Martí's historical background and is predisposed to be carried away by patriotic and personal emotions, the sadness of the child's eyes seems to augment the complexity of the emotional reaction to what is seen happening on the screen.

Moreover, if the reflections on the 1862 photo of Martí the child are placed into dialogue with Roland Barthes's *Camera Lucida*, it can be argued that the gallery and the conventions that surround the 1862 photo's subject form the *studium* or ambience around the image, and the boy's gaze represents the *punctum* or individual detail that moves us and in which the subject's humanity is concentrated. In other words, as far as the portrait is concerned, we exist in a complex relationship between the era's photographic conventions, the image of the sad eyes of Martí the child as a form of individual resistance to those conventions, and our own reaction to the whole phenomenon in the present. In the terminology of Walter Benjamin, the boy's sad gaze is an *auratic* expression as a reaction to a postauratic age, and this, I believe, is another historical and ontological connection between Martí's image in the photograph and its representation on the film (Benjamin 1969b; Duttlinger 2008). However, I believe that, in a certain way, our participation is even greater with the film than the photograph precisely because in addition to what we now know about the photographic image, we also react to the moving images and to the historical and familial contextualization created according to the cinematographic conventions of our day. This means that, due to the extreme technological development in our time, we who observe the visual representation of nineteenth-century Martí are part of the conventions of modernization and of modern technologies to an even greater degree than Martí himself. That is why I argue that this has to influence us, perhaps unconsciously, in our reaction to the sad eyes of the character of Martí the child in the film. All this implies that viewing the film is a semiconscious activity that includes technological aspects from Martí's era (our memory of his photographs) and our own (the cinematographic illusion in which we participate). This is also a participatory activity in the sense that we seem to react to the impression of individuality that we perceive in the person filmed and to our emotional charge that can barely resist the temptation of feeling, although momentarily and incompletely, as if what we see on the screen is real life. One could also conjecture that the sad gaze of the boy Martí, in the photograph and on screen, can be interpreted as a kind of rejection of the terrible world that was Cuba at the end of the nineteenth century, and perhaps it is also a rejection of our own world by ourselves. This all confirms that looking at this image establishes a *reciprocal dialogue* between observer and observed and the boy's sad-eyed and startled gaze (the eye of the canary?) is at least one of the main factors that contribute to the magic effect of the film. In conclusion, this reciprocal relationship between observed and observer implies a very complex imaginary empathy in today's interested observer.

A Political Gaze between Writing and the Visual Image

In *José Martí: The Eye of the Canary*, in consonance with Martí's ideas in his writings and speeches, there is an insistence on representing the transformation of the written word into political action. As a modernista, Martí's writing style was rather elaborate and elegant, but the importance he attributed to politics and elevated morality distanced him from other modernistas. His work was an attempt to integrate writing and political action.[7] That is why it is not surprising that at the very beginning of the film, before the narrative has begun, we see a handwriting on a sheet of paper, and this initial scene—an example of what Garrett Stewart calls "liminal shot"—serves as a persistent theme and as a "haunting trace of affective intensity" throughout the entire work (Stewart 2007; Hannabach 2010). Later in the film, we witness Martí's character (age 12 or 13) helping his father compose the official documents he must present to his superiors; an adolescent Martí is depicted translating the work of Lord Byron and other romantic writers at the home of his teacher; subsequent scenes show how the young man uses his pen for revolutionary activity; and finally, a later scene depicts how a compromising letter allows the authorities to condemn him to six years of prison (Figure 3.4). Therefore, the initial scene that might have appeared as a free-floating liminal shot, once we watch the entire movie we realize, retrospectively, that it was the first lead to the plot of the narrative: Martí's concept of discourse as an activity inseparable from life and political action. Also, the initial scene depicting the child Martí writing on a sheet of paper has a striking tactile feeling. In this liminal shot, we not only see a hand holding a pen while writing on a piece of paper but also hear a sound as if a metal pen is scratching the paper. As Garrett Stewart claims, in films the tactile effect of this type of initial shot usually reverberates throughout the work more affectively than just an initial step toward a narrative ending. This idea leads me to argue that the initial scene in *José Martí: The Eye of the Canary* is yet another subtle but effective mechanism of Pérez's technique to heighten not only the audience's gazing but also its other basic sensory (a scratching physical feeling in this case) reactions as well (Stewart 2007; Hannabach 2010).

A MELANCHOLIC GAZE BETWEEN PHOTOGRAPHY AND FILM

There are other complexities related to watching these images depicting Martí. As I argued in the introduction to this book, heroic iconography like that of Martí is always represented in what W. J. T. Mitchell calls "mixed media" (Mitchell 2005). We must not forget that Martí's images often appear inserted into historical and scholarly texts or alongside anthems, speeches, and flags. Additionally, as Mitchell proposes, all representations are *mixed* because, even a written text is really also a visual medium given that when we read we form visual images of what we read (Mitchell 2005). Mitchell's ideas lead to the conclusion that images form part of the structure of the written text and, therefore, visual image and language contaminate one another. Something similar and more immediately poignant occurs in the relationship between Martí's photographic image and the one we see moving on screen: one conditions the other in a visual juxtaposition that might lead to the emotional outpouring audiences are encouraged to experience upon seeing the film.

With all the semiotic systems that are implied around these images, it is not difficult to understand the strong emotions that an interested observer must feel when he or she watches this film. Although, as I mentioned before, Fernando Pérez departs from the original portrait in the casting of the film characters if we look— regardless how incomplete and nonmimetic—at the filmic images of the young Martí in prison while having the photographic images in mind (see Figures 1.3 and 1.4 and Figure 3.4 in this chapter), it is easy to understand how these two types of images may converge to evoke strong emotions when we watch the film. Despite the iconic differences between the filmic images and the original photograph, when the interested observer watches the filmic images

Figure 3.4   Film still of adolescent José Martí in prison, 2010

having the photo image in the back of our memory, is as if the still image has become the image of a living Martí moving in front of our eyes (Wollen 2003).

Those of us familiar with the historical circumstances around "prisoner 113" might remember the prison photograph alongside Martí's famous poem to his mother in which Martí aludes to his sacrifice for his country and his filial piety. Both the photographic image and the filmic image of the chained boy hearken back to the notion of martyrdom implied by all the prior and posterior history that converges in those images. Everything alluding to the images of "prisoner 113" is part of what Roberto Tejada calls the "ambientation of the image" (Tejada 2009, 8–18), the idea that every image is always surrounded by a discursive and experiential environment, and this is certainly part of the complex ambientation on the filmic image. Only by becoming conscious of these and other mediations is it possible to comprehend critically what we really see in the photograph of Prisoner 113 and in the film: how the images' production mechanisms have conditioned our way of reacting to them.

Another example of possible visual and emotional association between images in the film and previous photographic and pictorial images in our memory is the scene when the representation of boy Martí appears learning how to ride a horse (Figure 3.5). For a casual observer, this scene (played by the actor Damián Rodríguez) might seem rather unemotional or at least not very dramatic, but for the interested observer familiar with photographic and pictorial images of Martí, this scene, regardless of visual (dis)similarities, can conjure an emotional and historical association with the 1895 pictorial images of Martí mortally wounded and falling from his horse in Dos Ríos (see Figure 4.1 for an example). The pictorial image of Martí falling from his horse in the 1917 painting by Valderrama in Figure 4.1 in Chapter 4 is a good example of a possible dramatic retrospective association with the film scene in question.

Another of the most emotional moments of the film is near the end, when the father (who appears throughout the movie as a very severe and rough man who even strikes his son on occasion) kneels before the depiction of a chained Martí and, upon seeing the young

Figure 3.5   Film still in which Martí the child learns how to ride a horse, 2010

man's ankles swollen and shredded by his shackles, exclaims in hor-
ror, "But how can they do this? How is it possible that they've got
you like this?" Once the film has shown this dramatic scene between
father and son, there is a final still shot of the face of the actor who
plays teenage Martí looking intensely to the lens as if demanding a
strong reaction from us the spectators. From the technical point of
view, this final still shot is a reminder of the photographic origin of
nondigital films, but it is also a final ploy of the movie to demand
from us a strong emotional, ethical, and political reaction (Stewart
2007; Hannabach 2010). All these scenes heighten the emotions of
the interested observer and, simultaneously, obscure our reflective
capacity by making us believe that we see them objectively. After
all, the historical event does not cause the effect produced in us
when we look at these images, but rather this effect is conditioned
by the political and emotional exigencies of the present in the form
of its *retrospective reconstruction*.

As a final reflection about this film, we can say that the relationship between Martí's image and his disappearance from real
life invites us into a meditation on the psychoanalytical phenomenon of melancholia in which the photograph, like death, is characterized by immobility and silence but also tries to console us by
promising us a piece of the one who is gone. In other words, our
reaction to a canonical photo of Martí functions like the formation
of a fetish in the unconscious, since, on the one hand, it produces
a sensation of fixity and death, but on the other it allows us to
attempt to give life to the image that continues to reverberate and
produce effects in its observers.[8] For these reasons, the fact that the
film only represents Martí until the age of 17 avoids confronting
directly the ghost that haunts our melancholia: the tragic and early
death of the martyr-hero. All of this leads me to conclude that
the film repeatedly suggests a slippage between the moving film
image and the static photo image of Martí and vice versa. This
movement prevents us from completely accepting the intimate
relationship between the photograph and death. This means that
the gaze of Martí's photograph implies the search for a moving
image, while the film's images seek to immortalize the national hero

in a kind of photographical stillness. This is part of the complex dynamic of melancholia behind the feeling that we, Martí's admirers, are overcome with when we see this film with the memory of his previous photographs and paintings in the back of our minds. But the impact of the relationship between the film's moving image and the still photographic and pictorial images of the lost hero is perhaps just a limited visual account of our own strong emotion. It is a complex reaction that entails both a terrible feeling of victimhood and a fantasy of omnipotence; it is also a form of suffering that testifies to our acknowledgment of powerlessness in the face of the irreversibility of time and the fact that the real Martí will never be recuperated.[9] But, paradoxically, we have to still take into consideration that Martí's memory continues to be that of the most believable, most sincere, and most self-sacrificing martyr, and for that reason we are so willing to let ourselves be carried along by a reciprocal gaze that connects his image with our own present condition. Faced with such intellectual and emotional complexity, we latter-day *martianos* should not be surprised by our strong emotional reaction to *José Martí: The Eye of the Canary*.

CHAPTER 4

MELANCHOLIA FOR MARTÍ

CLEARLY PLAYING ON A METAPHOR OF A socially constructed domain of power, Sigmund Freud's reference to conscience as "among the major institutions of the ego" (Freud 1974, 243) suggests not only that conscience is instituted, produced, and maintained within a larger polity and its organizations but that the ego and its various parts are also accessible through a metaphorical language that attributes a social content and structure to these presumably psychic phenomena. Although Freud begins his essay "Mourning and Melancholia" by insisting on the indisputably "psychogenic nature" (Freud 1974, 243) of the melancholia and mourning under consideration in the essay, he also provides social metaphors that not only govern the topographic descriptions of melancholy's operation but also implicitly undo his own claim to provide a specifically psychogenic explanation of these psychic states (Butler 1997, 178).

A DEPATHOLOGIZED COLLECTIVE MELANCHOLIA

The cult of José Martí in the Cuban national narrative goes beyond an extended act of mourning for the loss of the national martyr-hero and is better understood as a social form of melancholia. In this chapter, I argue that the obsessive reproduction, dissemination, regulation, and veneration of Martí's visual images—exemplified in this chapter through film, photographs, drawings, and paintings—are attempts by people within the Cuban national narrative to express a sense of loss, seemingly unable to overcome their feeling of mourning. In other words, the Cuban iconographic obsession with Martí's image is symptomatic of Freudian melancholia and reflects several key tenets of the psychoanalytic concept as theorized by Judith Butler, David L. Eng, and David Kazanjian (Butler 1997; Eng and Kazanjian 2003a). Freudian psychoanalysis indicates that in the process of mourning, the passionate force that unites the mourner with the lost object (the image of the deceased Martí in this case) wishes to die with it; nevertheless, the survival instinct demands the right to keep living. If mourning for the lost object is to be overcome, the nature of one's feeling about the missing object must be transformed: one gradually learns to accept the object as dead instead of continuing to desire its living presence, ignoring reality's verdict and therefore prolonging the intensity of suffering. In this understanding of mourning, the subject also susbstitutes new objects of affection for the lost object.

While Freud at times wavers between pathologization and universalism in his description of melancholia, my interpretation resists such pathologization and understands melancholia as more akin to what Eng and Kazanjian explain in the introduction to *Loss*: "[W]e find in Freud's conception of melancholia's persistent struggle with its lost objects not simply a 'grasping' and 'holding' on to a fixed notion of the past but rather a continuous engagement with loss and its remains. This engagement generates sites of memory and history. While mourning abandons lost objects by laying their histories to rest, melancholia's continued and open relations to the past finally allows us to gain new perspectives on and new understanding of lost objects" (Eng and Kazanjian 2003b, 4).

They expand their view of a revised melancholia by connecting it to Butler's:

Ultimately, we learn, the work of mourning is not possible without melancholia. [. . .] In *The Ego and the Id* (1923), Freud comes to this conclusion by understanding that the ego is constituted through the remains of abandoned object-cathexes. As a psychic entity, the ego is composed of the residues of its accumulated losses. In *The Psychic Life of Power*, Judith Butler expands upon this revised notion of melancholia, arguing that the incorporative logic of melancholia founds the very possibility of the ego and its psychic topography. [. . .] Put otherwise, melancholia is the precondition for both the ego and the work of mourning [. . .] melancholia creates a realm of traces open to signification, a hermeneutic domain of what remains of loss. (Eng and Kazanjian 2003b, 4)

This definition of mourning implies that in order for the subject to be "cured," it has to abandon its engagement with the lost object. But Butler and Eng and Kazanjian's revised definition of melancholia—which I am subscribing to here—conceives it as an open relation to the past in such a way that allows the subject to gain a new insight on the lost object.

What I argue in this chapter, then, is not for a process of mourning that ultimately forgets Martí (that would be an undesirable impossibility) but for a social and depathologized form of melancholia that, by taking advantage of its persisting affective attachment to the loss of the ideals represented by Martí's image, opens new creative connections between the past and the present. Like mourning, this interpretation of melancholia attempts to free the ego from the fixed passion for the lost loved object, while such interpretation also opens up our connection with the lost object to new relationships between memories and histories and between the dead and the living.

In what follows, I argue that the extensive reproduction and dissemination of Martí's images suggest that many Cubans immersed within the national narrative—faced with the loss of Martí and with the implied loss of the high ideals he represented in the national narrative, as well as the social and political disappointment after his death—tend to recoil their affective energy toward Martí's iconography instead of transforming it into a process that would allow them to be free from a fixed passionate attachment, a process that would unlock other national possibilities and discourses. Again, it is not a question of rejecting or denying "Martí" but rather a call to resignify his memory, to unleash other possibilities for relationship between past and present by means of the same psychic forces that initially fixed his image in the Cuban narrative. I argue that this process of resignification seems only possible through a depathologized form of melancholia that has to include our capacity for critical agency.

THE DEATH OF A BUREAUCRAT

The character of Tío Paco in Tomás Gutiérrez Alea's (1928–1996) Cuban movie *La muerte de un burócrata* (The Death of a Bureaucrat; 1966), a darkly comedic and biting critique of Cuban government bureaucracy, can be illuminating for my argument. I call this figure the "Tío Paco metaphor" because Tío Paco represents the compulsive Cuban fascination for Martí's image in this film. Tío Paco, I argue, is a social metaphor for a psychic configuration that is formed by the melancholic withdrawal from external reality. Moreover, this melancholic formation only has the possibility of moving away from this state by the energy of the critical agency that is in conflict with the tendency to fix the object within the topography of the ego, and that is precisely what I want to deploy in my study. The Tío Paco metaphor demonstrates that with the loss of such passionate attachment or cathexis that many Cubans seem to have with the nationalist image of Martí, only the critical agency formed in our psychic topography can return this passionate attachment to a topography that would allow new possibilities of social resignification.

In *La muerte de un burócrata*, Gutiérrez Alea addresses the extreme—almost morbid—obsession of many Cubans with Martí's image and its possible consequences. In the film's narrative, Tío Paco—an exemplary worker—dies in a workplace accident and is buried with his union card as symbol of his admirable proletarian dedication. The plot gets complicated when Tío Paco's widow attempts to collect his pension and discovers her serious error: her husband's credential is required to collect her state benefits. The rest of the film's narrative centers on Tío Paco's nephew and his multiple and obsessive attempts to recover his uncle's card and the frustrations generated by the country's bureaucracy, which not only prevents the nephew from resolving the problem but also causes his every move to complicate and undermine his efforts. None of this would seem to be of particular interest for my thesis if not for the fact that Tío Paco's death was due to his patriotic invention: a machine for mass-producing busts of Martí. The noble impulse behind the machine's creation was to put a bust in the home of every Cuban family. Unfortunately for Tío Paco, the invention broke down and, when he went to fix it, he fell into the machinery and became a victim of his own patriotic obsession. In fact, the last bust that comes out of the machine after the accident is made with a mixture of clay and Tío Paco's own body.

The dark comedy unites some problematic elements of Cuban nationhood: the suffering and frustration of citizens faced with an intolerable bureaucracy and the obsession with the reproduction and dissemination of Martí's image and its consequences. My point here is that the tragicomic situation in *La muerte de un burócrata* has implications that go far beyond the repeated criticisms of Cuba's bureaucracy. Tío Paco's Martían obsession with making sure every family has a bust of the apostle is far from a simple joke or fictional representation, unconnected to a national discourse. Actually, the film's plot represents the problems caused by both bureaucracy and extreme patriotic responses to the cult of Martí. That is why I propose that both these elements—bureaucracy and extreme devotion to Martí's iconicity—are in fact two sides of the same coin: the exaggerated repetition of the martyr's image is directly related to the failures of national politics not only during the time of the film's plot but also since the Cuban Republic's beginnings in the early twentieth century.

THE REPUBLICAN VACUUM

As mentioned, one of the two sides of the Tío Paco metaphor is the social and political disillusionment that may cause some Cubans to recoil inward as a protective reaction against a negative reality. My argument in this chapter and throughout the book takes into consideration that constant crises continued in Cuba after the end of Spanish colonial domination in 1898. Among the most obvious post-Spanish colonization crises include US military interventions and neocolonial control, corrupt local governments, cruel dictatorships, and a radical revolution, which caused a large part of the population to go into exile. From here comes, I argue, the melancholic formation that fetishizes Martí. The idea of Martí becomes a creed as an attempt—always frustrated by the social and political contingecies—by the Cuban national narrative to overcome a lack in the life of its citizens. This is the reason Martí is seen as more than a hero and more than a martyr in Cuba (and in Cuban communities everywhere); he is also seen as a kind of redeeming saint to whose ubiquitous image constant devotion must be performed. The nineteenth-century Cuban project of national liberation was grounded in the paradigm of martyrdom, of dying for one's country, and Martí fit perfectly into this redemptive role. Throughout Cuban history, this paradigm has been represented in many ways, including through the use of visual icons, which are compulsively reproduced by all kinds of cultural institutions. In the rendering of these images, Martí's life and work are fundamental, but so is his martyrdom, which occupies a privileged and unique place on Cuba's altar of patriotic heroes (Rojas 2006). An entire redemptive national teleology has been built around his image in an attempt to fill what several Cuban historians and intellectuals have characterized as a republican gap that challenges a national sense of fulfillment (Rojas 2008b).

Such an endemic critical situation demanded that the nation be rescued and reconstituted using Martí's ideals as the principal means to that end. This is one reason this redemptive narrative has been so effectively used by the Cuban Left—especially when articulated by Fidel Castro himself. This narrative proposes that only a radical shift toward socialism, and therefore away from the republican capitalist past, can reconstruct the national telos created by Martí, which was lost during the Cuban Republic and supposedly restored in 1959 when Castro came to power. From his earliest appearance on the political stage, Castro insisted that Martí was the intellectual author of his political movement.[1] At that time, most of the country was ready to embrace this revolutionary teleology.

The sense of republican emptiness and defeat, combined with a version of Martísm that favored Castro's political agenda is, in my opinion, one of the main reasons behind both the extraordinary popular support that the revolution received in 1959 and the long duration of the Castros' government even after the fall of the Soviet Union in the early 1990s.

A PERSONAL HEROIC LEGACY

It should be recalled that José Martí imagined a Cuban nationality from exile, mostly in the United States. He lived in Cuba for only the first 17 years of his life (1853–1871), plus a few short months toward the end of the 1870s, and a few weeks before his death in Dos Ríos in 1895. In his exilic activities, writings, and speeches, Martí tried to construct an ideal image of the future Cuban nation. These activities included—as I have discussed in Chapter 1—the construction of his own visual image, which reflected his desire to foment a sense of national unity around his leadership and sense of personal martyrdom.

We should not overlook the fact that Martí's persona and personal history lends itself well to a redemptive narrative that suggests implicitly or explicitly that his image can symbolically overcome the moral and political gap left by the failed Cuban Republic. As such, it is instructive to recount here some of the most salient of Martí's political actions that have become part of his heroic mystique. To begin Cuba's last war of independence Martí organized the La Fernandina expedition, which failed because of a last-minute betrayal that caused the US government to interrupt what would have been three simultaneous invasions of Cuba. But a few months after this enormous failure, in early 1895, Martí—who was living at the time in New York—went off to war alongside General Máximo Gómez (the military leader of Cuba's independence movement) and a small number of insurrectionaries. On this occasion, not even Máximo Gómez could dissuade him from participating in a struggle (for which he was poorly equipped—Martí's health was fairly weak and he had no previous military experience) and joining Gómez and other revolutionaries in what would be the final struggle for independence from Spain.

Between January 30 (when he left New York) and May 19 (the day he was mortally wounded), Martí carried out a truly frenetic campaign. He left New York on January 30 to Cap-Haïtien (on Haiti's northern coast), and from here he went to meet General Máximo Gómez in Montecristi (a region in the northern Dominican Republic), where he and Máximo Gómez wrote and signed the Montecristi Manifesto, the official document of the Cuban Revolutionary Party. On April 1, he left for Cuba with Gómez and four other companions; and on April 11, after several stops along the way, they sighted Cuba and that night the six expeditionaries rowed to shore at a place called Playitas in southeastern Cuba. That night they slept on the ground close to where they disembarked. On April 14, they met with the region's guerrilla fighters. During the next several days they climbed through the hills, marched along a river, received word from other guerrilla groups fighting in the area, camped in the wilderness, and slept in shacks until April 25 when they entered the Guantánamo region and heard the shots from José Maceo's group who were fighting the Spanish. On that occasion, Martí helped heal some wounded fighters. Over the next few days Gómez, Martí, J. Maceo, and the troops set up camp, and Martí used this time to write instructions, dispatch correspondence, and rally the troops. On May 2, they reached an encampment where Martí met with *New York Herald* correspondent George Eugene Bryson. The next day, Martí wrote a manifesto letter that was sent to the newspaper. May 5 was an important day for this struggle because Gómez and Martí were summoned to a meeting by Antonio Maceo (the war's highest military commander). It is said that A. Maceo and Martí had serious disagreements in this meeting, because while Martí proposed an assembly of revolutionary delegates to manage the war effort, A. Maceo preferred a more traditional military junta.

After the meeting, Gómez and Martí continued up the Cauto River, where they camped in an abandoned ranch called Dos Ríos. It rained continually for three days, and on May 17, Gómez left with forty riders to harass a Spanish convoy. That same day, Martí remained in charge of the camp with twenty men, while Gómez carried out his battle plan. On May 19, Martí sent a message to Goméz, notifying him of the arrival of General Masó and his cavalry. Gómez returned to camp, never having encountered the Spanish forces. A few minutes later, Cuban scouts reported that the Spanish convoy was approaching the camp, having followed Gómez's trail. Gómez rushed to attack with several horsemen, ordering Martí to leave camp. The Spanish forces repelled Gómez's attack, who ordered new charges against them.

The official version of this fateful moment says that while Gómez was trying to repel the Spanish troops, Martí and the young soldier Ángel de la Guarda charged the enemy and both were wounded, mortally in Martí's case. But another version of the tragedy insists that Martí never charged; rather, Martí and his companion became confused amid the gun battle and ended up by mistake among the enemy soldiers, who shot Martí three times, mortally wounding him. The Cubans were unable to rescue Martí's body, which was taken to Remanganaguas to be identified. It was then taken to Santiago de Cuba, where it was displayed and finally buried on May 27 in Santa Ifigenia Cemetery. On February 24, 1907, Martí's remains were transferred to a modest pantheon, and from September 1947 to June 1951, they were housed provisionally in the Tableau of Heroes before finally being interred in a new mausoleum on June 30, 1951 (Martí 1975c, 27:204–9).

A REALIST PAINTING

It is indisputable that the visual impact of Martí's iconography would have been greatly enhanced if we had pictures of him during his insurrection activities from the moment of his departure from Cap-Haïtien to the day of his death in Two Rivers. However, in May 1894, just a few months before going to war in Cuba, Martí had one of his last pictures taken during his life. In the photograph, he appears next to his friend, Fermín Valdés Domínguez, who reportedly asked Martí why they were not taking the photo in the Cuban countryside. Martí, in his usual martyrdom tone, responded, "We're going there to die, not to take pictures" (Hernández Serrano 2009). It is rather paradoxical that despite the fact that Martí was so aware of the advances of photography of the second part of the nineteenth century, and the fact that from the time he was imprisoned during his teenage years he used photography to enhance the image he wanted to project of himself, he rejected the possibility of making use of it in the most crucial moment of his political and military activities. There is also a certain irony in Martí's refusal given the fact that by 1895—the year of Martí's death—Kodak had begun to sell a portable camera that allowed photo reporters to take the camera out of the studio and onto the battlefield. Martí, however, never made use of this technology despite his great interest in photography and his obvious determination to control the way his visual image was projected. These two historical phenomena—the new Kodak and Martí's battlefield protagonism in Cuba—could have coincided; the fact that they did not has denied us an enormously rich visual drama.[2]

In the absence of battlefield photographs, some painters and artists turned to realistic painting styles in an attempt to capture as much as possible the indexical potential of the Martí's image. Figure 4.1, a reproduction of a realist-style painting of Martí's death in Dos Ríos, is an example of the early artistic interest in constructing a myth of Martí through his realistic visual image. I also want to emphasize the importance of the extent to which Esteban Valderrama went to try to capture a "realistic" image of what could have been Martí falling from his horse at the moment of been wounded. Again, it seems to be that the realistic style employed by the painter indicates an enormous effort to capture of a piece of the "real" Martí.

In order to describe the lengths to which Valderrama went in attempting a "realistic" style, I translate the following paragraph from Arturo R. Carricarte's explanation,

> Señor Valderrama's artistic scruples are so strict that, in addition to researching as much as he could, he went to Dos Ríos and lodged there;

Figure 4.1   *La muerte de Martí en Dos Ríos* (Martí's Death in Two Rivers) by
Esteban Valderrama, 1917

all of his sketches were done at the hour of the Apostle's tragic fall, with the model placed in the position that biographers say Martí occupied, using the light at the proper angle. He also chose the month of May, despite the rains and propensity for plague in our countryside. Poorly lodged, with every difficulty of transportation, he carried out his work with no other ambition or motive than his artistic fervor and great love for the Master, and with no intention of profit.[3]

What we know about this painting shows the obsessive insistence of at least some Cuban artists of the time with precision and realistic detail reproducing his image. This style of realistic painting compensates for the lack of photographs of this traumatic moment. It is a clear illustration of the painter's effort to make Martí's death and the visual image of his wounded body a fetish that can somehow indexically stand in for Martí's material body and reality.

Despite Valderrama's enormous effort to adhere to realism in his representation, critics were not positive in their assessment of his painting's exactitude. In what follows, I translate Jorge Bermúdez explanation of this issue:

Created in 1917, [the painting] represented Valderrama in the 1918 Salón de Bellas Artes. Nevertheless, critics were unfavorable toward it, pointing out some historical inexactitudes that took little or nothing away from the work. But it was enough to make the great academic painter's pride destroy it. As a consequence, the only color visual proof of its existence is a trichrome that the magazine *Bohemia* had published on its cover (February 24, 1918) as the commemoration of the beginning of the War of 1895 coincided with the opening of the aforementioned Salón; using this image, Valderrama's canvas was digitally restored for this *Antología visual*, 85 years after its exposition and subsequent destruction.[4]

In the accounts previously mentioned, it is easy to notice both the painter's dedication to Martí's realistic memory and critics' attacks against the canvas precisely for not being realistic enough. Both the painter's and critics' extraordinary concern with realism exemplifies an early tendency to represent Martí as Christlike, a figure who must be recuperated or revived at least iconographically; the memory of Martí's corporeal remains should be preserved at all costs. The information about Valderrama's painting as well as the historical details about Martí's life and death contributes to our understanding of the mystique that surrounds Martí's image. This fascination has been repeated and enlarged in Cuban culture to the point of creating a truly extraordinary mystification of enormous proportions that implies, in my view, a feeling of melancholia.

ESCHATOLOGY OF THE MARTYR

Another revealing aspect of Martí's national sanctification process and of the melancholia some Cubans seem to feel around his loss is the obsessive attention paid in Cuban media to every detail related to Martí's corpse from the moment he was shot until the burial and reinterment of his remains. Such obsessive media attention to detail is exemplified in Jorge Oller Oller's 2010 article "Historia de las fotos que corroboraron la muerte de José Martí" ("History of the Photos that Corroborated José Martí's Death"; Oller Oller). In addition to providing information about the photos of Martí's corpse, Oller Oller's article is essentially an eschatology of a martyr. Its detail is such that it appears to deal with the body of a saint that has been buried, dug up, and buried again. The excessive mortuary detail gives a vivid and morbid account of Martí's traveling corpse from the moment he is killed to after he is buried and reburied. The first thing the article mentions is that after the news of his death in May 1895, some Cuban patriots in New York doubted that Martí was really dead and only accepted the terrible verdict after being told about the personal effects Martí had with him when he was killed. Among these effects was a portrait of his daughter María Mantilla (the article claims she is only his goddaughter), which was known only to a few of Martí's closest friends. This information is so engulfed in details about the corpse that it seems like an excuse for the author to provide countless other details about what happened during the hours, days, and weeks following Martí's fall in Dos Ríos. At the end of the long and extremely detailed article,

Oller Oller states that on May 27, the military governor of the city of Santiago de Cuba arranged for Martí's burial to be protected by strict military security. Moments earlier, some Cubans and a Spanish captain, a friend of Martí, asked to be allowed to identify the body. The petition was granted and the casket was opened. Higinio Martínez, the photographer from the paper *La Caricatura* (The Caricature), took a snapshot of the corpse. Then the very colonel whose troops had killed Martí laid the body to rest with some rather laudatory remarks. Oller Oller's retelling continues, revealing information about what happened during the burial and subsequent days and weeks leading up to July 17 of that year.

About the photograph of Martí's deceased body, Oller Oller quotes the photographer Higinio Martínez's letter to *La Caricatura*. Here is my translation from Martínez's letter:

> Although the photograph was taken—eight days after death [. . .] in the battle of Dos Ríos, and despite the progress of rapid decomposition due to the humidity of the ground, everyone recognized the revolutionary, señor Martí, because death's hand has not yet had the time to erase the distinctive features of his physiognomy. The broad forehead that gave his visage such a unique stamp, the curly hair, and other signs on his body exactly match the photos we've all seen and the records submitted by family members, so that the cadaver has been properly identified. At the same time, I remit to you photographs of the cemetery, the coffin in which he was taken from Remanganaguas, and the niche where he now lies in the Necropolis.[6]

Such a gruesome image of Martí's head separated from the rest of his body can be understood as a metaphor for the Cuban sense of a collapse of his vision of the world and of the Cuban Republic and the consequent implied responsibility of his followers (of diverse political stripes) to somehow repair this mystic body that has been torn apart and dispersed. At times, when reading Oller Oller's entire account, it seems as if it is describing the details of a Christlike being who, after his crucifixion, might at any time resuscitate. Most of the details of this article, due to their excessive and

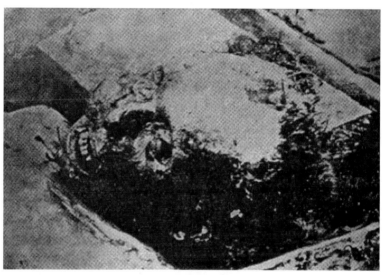

Figure 4.2   The head of the deceased José Martí, 1895[5]

morbid descriptions, are yet another expression of a profound sense of melancholia for the loss of the martyr-hero.

COMPULSIVE AND COMPULSORY ICONOLATRY

As historian Lillian Guerra explains, Martí's iconography was not only compulsive but compulsory:

> In June of 1921, a group of Conservative lawmakers, largely from [the provinces of] Santa Clara and Matanzas, presented a bill to the Cuban House of Representatives that would make José Martí's birthday, January 28th, a national holiday. It passed with overwhelming support. Known as "The Law that Glorifies the Apostle," the law required that all municipalities dedicate not only a principal street in every town to Martí but also "a statue, bust, obelisk, commemorative column, bronze plaque, or stone tablet" in whatever public space was deemed most appropriate. Furthermore, the law ordered that annually, at exactly eight o'clock in the morning on the day of Martí's birth, all schoolchildren in Cuba "with a flower on their breast . . . offer an affectionate tribute to José Martí" at this commemorative site. Accompanied by local citizens, the children were then asked to recite verses, sing hymns, and listen to the "panegyrics" of one or more speakers. (Guerra 2006, 34)

In fact, anyone who has traveled to the island will have likely noticed that Martí's image is found at every turn in busts, paintings, wall sketches, posters, statues, pamphlets, books, television shows, wax museums, and all kinds of monuments. Even beyond the capital (and even outside the national territory, for that matter), reproductions of Martí's image are more evident than his ideas in many Cuban communities. For example, in US photographer Alex Harris's 2007 book *The Idea of Cuba*, a significant number of the images show busts of Martí. These appear in both obvious and obscure places throughout the island: in government buildings, parks, highways, streets, patios, bus stops, small shops, private living rooms, and corners overgrown by grass and bushes. The section titled "Martí" takes up 30 of the book's 134 pages, and although the other pages contain photographs of old cars, crumbling buildings, attractive young Cubans, and monuments, it is noteworthy that in addition to the section dedicated entirely to busts of Martí, other images of the apostles appear throughout the rest of the book.

Harris begins his preface by noting, "When I landed at José Martí airport in Havana in the spring of 1998, I knew nothing about Martí. Now I see that his ideas—even his persona—were already present in my work," and ends the introduction declaring, "Over a century after [Martí's] death, it must be clear to most Cubans that neither Martí's utopian idea of Cuba nor the exemplary socialist state promised by Castro will ever be achieved. But what Martí calls his 'errant love' has—perhaps with the help of angels—found a resting place in the hearts of Cubans. José Martí has given Cubans the one essential feeling necessary for human progress. He has given them hope" (Harris *Idea of Cuba*, 38). It is instructive to point out here how, in spite of the fact that Harris confesses that just a few short years before publishing *The Idea of Cuba* he knew absolutely nothing about Martí, he concludes the preface in a mystical tone. This suggests that Harris has already been "converted" into a passionate admirer of Martí, and that he now is contributing to the mystification of the Cuban national hero through the reproduction of his images and through the enthusiastic declaration that Martí's "errant love" "has—perhaps with the help of angels—found a resting place in the hearts of Cubans."

Since Martí's death, Cuban patriots and politicians from every ideological persuasion have used his image for their political agendas. The need for a national martyrdom myth reveals the desire to repair the hole left by what several historians and intellectuals consider the lack of an organic, noncolonial national tradition. Martí's iconography (specifically that which refers to the meaning of his death and "resurrection") has supported a symbolic recovery of what could have been but was not. This is what the nation is imagined to have become if Martí himself—or his uncorrupted ideals—had guided the nation after its independence from Spain (Rojas 2006).

Figure 4.3   Cuba Libre weeping at José Martí's tomb, 1907

"The icon of Cuba Libre weeping at Martí's tomb on the anniversary of the Grito de Baire, or call to arms, for the 1895 War. The image reflects the mood of many Cubans after the collapse of the Constitutional Revolution of 1906 led to a second US military occupation" (From *El Fígaro* cover, February 24, 1907; Guerra 2005, 195).

Figure 4.4   Mary Magdalene weeping at José Martí's feet, 1900

"An example of the early imagery of Martí as Cuba's messiah. This image, accompanied by Martí's love poem to a young woman, features the icon of Cuba Libre, cast in the role of Mary Magdalene, weeping at his feet" (From *El Fígaro*, March 11, 1900, 111; Guerra 2005, 195).

Another prevalent trend in plastic arts representations of Martí is the painting of his death as heroic, surrounded with nationalist symbols. Cuban visual media are one of the main agents of Cuban collective memory, and many paintings and drawings about Martí (in particular those that represent his death) represent him not as a completely dead man but as a resurrected or "resurrectable," Christlike hero.

SPECIAL PERIOD: MEMORIALIZATION AND HERESY

It is in the latter part of the twentieth century during the so-called Special Period, the critical moment after the 1991 fall of the Soviet Union and the loss of its financial and military support of the island, that the Cuban government greatly intensified the "museification" of the nation, including that of Martí's iconography. This museification is rather paradoxical: faced with the great crisis of the 1990s the state actively promoted museums to preempt social instability. However, at the same time, some young Cuban artists adopt a nonconformist position toward the representation of Martí's figure. I argue that this nonconformist approach to the representation of Martí's figure, without rejecting or denying the image of Martí, is a sign of the critical possibilities of national melancholia.

In response to the devastating economic instability in the Special Period, the Cuban government emphasized a "cultural nationalism"—in contrast to the previous internationalist Che Guevara's "new man" position—in which Martí's cult is more central and crucial than ever before (Hernandez-Reguant 2009b). This time the revolution, instead of emphasizing the future, emphasized the past, specifically looking backward to the revolution's own achievements. The term *Special Period* was Castro's claim that this was a hiatus in which what was supposed to be a straight line of prosperity had temporally collapsed. As Rachel Weiss says in *To and from Utopia in the New Cuban Art*, during the 1990s Cuba saw an enormous increase in new museums—seventy new museums were built between 1996 and 2004 alone. Weiss makes several important observations about this issue: "Cuba had never been translated, repeated, so often. Translation, repetition: phenomena constellated around the need to hold something fast, to recuperate something that has been lost. The repetition machine of the museum remade Cuba's coherent, comprehensible, and valorous: museums are, in their way, little utopias, ideal versions unassailable in their logic and completeness, and now the Museum Cuba had replaced the Utopia Cuba" (Weiss 2011).

Jonathan Dettman, building on Weiss's formulation, points out that the museum serves at least three corresponding functions: As an archive of cultural artifacts and memories, (1) it preserves the island's past; (2) it configures history according to the particular ideological coordination of the present and performs an educative function in line with the state's official version of the people, places, and events of the past; and (3) the museum generates income (Dettman forthcoming).

It is worth mentioning in this regard that in spite of Castro's effort to identify his revolution and his own persona with that of Martí's, it was not until 1996 that the official museum memorial in honor of Martí was finally dedicated by the Castro government at the base of the José Martí Memorial in the Revolution Plaza. Because the Special Period marks the Castro government's greatest financial and political crisis, once again, one witnesses an increased interest in the official construction of Martí's iconography as an attempt at political unity and state control. It marks another attempt to create an imagined heroic national unity precisely at moments when state power becomes unstable. This time, however, the pendulum of biographical information included in the memorial swings decidedly toward Martí's anti-imperialism (Gonçalves 2006, 27–32).

DESACRALIZATION

There is a paradox in the Cuban government's museification of Martí however that became obvious in 1995, the centennial of Martí's death. In this year, the Cuban government created the Consejo Nacional de Patrimonio Cultural (National Counsel of

Cultural Patrimony). Additionally, it was in this same year that a series of paintings of what some scholars consider a "heretic" image of Martí began to appear in art events (Camacho 2003; Bermúdez 2004, 42). In his article "Los herejes en el convento: La recepción de José Martí en la plástica y la crítica cubana de los años 80 y 90" ("The Heretics in the Convent: The Reception of José Martí in the Cuban Plastic Arts and Criticism of the 1980s and 1990s"), Jorge Camacho argues that at the end of the 1980s and beginning of the 1990s Cuban plastic arts produced a series of artistic projects rethinking the figure of Martí from a critical point of view. For my analysis, Camacho's observation has validity, although I prefer to stay away from the assertion of the intentionality of these artists themselves. Whether these "heretic" pictorial representations of Martí were intentional or not is something I have not been able to corroborate.

I will only use two examples of paintings that appeared in Cuba in 1995 to suggest that in these pieces there is a *nonconformist* representation of Martí's heroic figure: Aimée García's *Sin título* (Untitled, 1995) (Figure 4.5), and Reinerio Tamayo Fonseca's *Me duele Cuba* (Cuba Hurts; 1995) (Figure 4.6).These pieces represent two different styles and reflect possible ideological deviations from the heroic and saintly representation of the figure of Martí.

In *Sin título*, Martí is represented with traits of European modernism or even decadentism. The subject is profiled elegantly in a relaxed seated position next to fashionable curtains, ostentatiously dressed in a silk shirt, and staring at a sphinx with a look more inquisitive than resolved. Pastel colors dominate (for an analysis of this painting, see Camacho 2003, 7). There is an important contrast between the visual image of Martí offered to us by this oil painting and Herman Norrman's portrait of Martí in New York in 1891. In Norrman's painting the subject appears sitting as if on the edge of the chair, looking forward energetically, with bookshelves in the background. Strong colors—red, yellow, and black—are in evidence. Norrman's painting is definitely on the side of heroic energy, while García's accentuates some sort of decadentism. More than a proletarian or a revolutionary, García's Martí looks like an

Figure 4.5 *"Untitled* by Aimée García, 1995"

aristocratic decadent dandy, and such this image distances Martí from his more conformist depictions. Aimée García can be considered part of a new generation of plastic artists that by 1995 had begun to imagine other, nonconformist images of the apostle.[7]

In *Me duele Cuba*, Martí appears short of stature and with a disproportionately large head. This can be taken as a reference to the well-known preponderance of head and forehead in Martí's traditional iconography, but the figure's open shirt reveals his entrails. This somewhat grotesque detail distances the representation of Martí from the idealized image of the hero's body. Although it differs greatly from García's painting, Tamayo's work is rather desacralizing. These and several other nonconformist paintings from this period present a basic contrast, because official iconography upheld an ideologically favorable vision in support of the regime, but on the other hand, it is in precisely the same moment that some plastic artists dare to give their work clearly heretical nuances (Bermúdez 2004, 39–47). This is why I claim that there are two contrasting sides of this phenomenon: faced with the great crisis of the 1990s, the state increased its promotion of an official interpretation of Martí's iconography in order to preempt social instability; at the same time, some young artists adopted a nonconformist position against a regime that has appropriated Martí's iconography to maintain the state's power in the face of the destabilizing blows it received from within and without the country. The nonconformist images of the Special Period suggest that there is a movement toward a resignification of Martí's image, and I argue that that would be a signal of a new insight acquired as part of the melancholia for Martí.

CONCLUSION

In the Cuban national narrative, Martí's death has been constructed as a traumatic rupture in the very center of the Cuban national teleology. The compulsive repetition of his image is a response that attempts but fails to fill the gap caused by a deep political frustration, to placate those people suffering from the trauma of a political

Figure 4.6 *"Me duele Cuba*, by Reinerio Tamayo Fonseca, 1995"

violation that cannot be completely repaired. This endless political uproar, in relation to the cult of Martí's image, is a phenomenon that can be approached from the point of view of the psychoanalytic processes of mourning and melancholia.[8]

Given the nationalist insistence on representing Martí only in heroic and saintly terms, the saturation of Martí's images (in Cuba, Miami, and anywhere there is a Cuban community) reflects a national melancholia for the loss of the heroic Martí. This complex and traumatic phenomenon bears on both the desire to fill an absence with a living presence and the transformation of an image into a collective icon. This icon becomes a kind of fetish that attempts to fill the hole caused by the memory of the physical disappearance of the martyr-hero. The excesses of this melancholic phenomenon implies that Martí is still alive, or at least still living in us, that he must be honored constantly and at times compulsorily, that his memory requires an almost religious reaction from us, that Martísm is something sacred and should never be questioned. I argue, therefore, that this compulsive obsession with reproducing Martí's image is a display of unresolved mourning, of a collective national melancholia. Only by attempting critical views of Martí's iconicity can we aspire to see it anew, to resignify it.

The constant excess of Martí's tense and contradictory reverberation is what leads me to propose that Cuban mourning for the absent martyr-hero has not been resolved. In addition, such excess is due to a national sense of emptiness that always returns with the unquestionable demand of an unfulfilled duty. This unconscious feeling of demand and this sense of national emptiness create fertile ground for national leaders to mobilize these sentiments for specific political ends, especially for forms of state control of the citizens in unstable political moments.

Despite official attempts, however, some painters and artists in the Special Period are providing a critical resignification of Martí's image. Instead of the ultimately consuming and deadly obsession of Tío Paco mentioned at the beginning of the chapter—the film character of *La muerte de un burócrata* whose desire to reproduce Martí's image eventually led to his gruesome end—some Special

Period painters and artists have resisted this demand and expressed critical new images of Martí. With this gesture they are helping, in my opinion, to open up other possibilities of the meanings and gazes of the memory of Martí and of the nation. Given this possibility, perhaps we should remember Freud's observation in "Mourning and Melancholia" when he said that people who suffer melancholia have a "keener eye for truth than other people who are not melancholic [. . .] we only wonder why man has to be ill before he can be accessible to a truth of this kind" (Freud 1974, 246).

RESISTING CUBAN
MELANCHOLIA

I HAVE CLAIMED THROUGHOUT THIS BOOK THAT the sense of loss manifested in the obsessive reproduction and dissemination of Martí's icons signals an unresolved sense of mourning, a morbid fascination with the lack that such a loss produces. But instead of trying to overcome that sense of mourning by attempting to *forget Martí* (an undesirable and impossible objective), we should use the traces of his memory as a utopic impulse toward forms of creative alternatives. When Martí's images are seen with a mystifying reverence, they maintain their hegemonic aura. That is why I argue that we should keep some degree of *critical* distance from those representations to overcome what I perceive as the present melancholia for Martí, as this might open up a space for resignifying Martí and, by extension, the nation. This process is precisely what I term *resisting Cuban melancholia*.

The possibility of resisting a collective melancholia by means of the critical insight invested within melancholia itself has been articulated before by other scholars and theoreticians.

In the following quote Wendy Brown—commenting on Benjamin's idea on the relationship between politics and melancholia—makes a clear connection between the melancholia of a political group (what she refers simply as the "Left") and the possibility that that same melancholia has to invest in political transformation: "In Benjamin's enigmatic insistence on the political value of a dialectical grasp of 'the time of the Now,' Left melancholia represents not only a refusal to come to terms with the particular character of the present, that is, a failure to understand history in terms other than 'empty time' or 'progress.' It signifies as well a certain narcissism with regard to one's past political attachments and identity that exceeds any contemporary investment in political mobilization, alliance, or transformation" (2003, 458–59).

Charity Scribner, in a similar line of thinking as Brown's, makes the claim that Walter Benjamin, surely a thinker with melancholic tendencies, offers one of his most important insights when he proposes that the melancholic feeling projected back onto failures and disappointments should not be an occasion of a weakening fixation on the past but rather a source of redemptive hope (2003, 308). This is also one of David Eng and David Kazanjian's main arguments in *Loss*, where they propose "that a better understanding of melancholic attachments to loss might depathologize those attachments making visible not only their social bases but also their creative unpredictable, political aspects" (2003b, 3).

My reliance upon reworking Freudian melancholia might be understood to conflate the workings of the mind and of Cuban society in general. However, building on postcolonial and critical race scholarship on national melancholia, I instead aim to call attention to decisive points at which a critical analysis can discover, in the construction and dissemination of Martí's icons, a feeling of guilt and unresolved mourning, a melancholia that demands for someone or something to repair the absence of the martyr-hero, a trauma that has its symbolic center in the Martí myth. Nor do I intend to imply a search for a single and undeniable historical "truth," which is why I think an analysis of memory, rather than historiography, is the key that may serve to unlock the unreflexive national fascination with Martí's iconography. If history aspires to an objective truth about the past, memory revisits the problematic by placing it immediately in the present via a retrospective reconstruction that always remains incomplete in the sense that it is not objective but nevertheless is valuable for what it says about what matters, in the present, to the subject in question.

The archival examples I have examined throughout this book imply not one but several Cuban national narratives—which, on the one hand, demand at times a utopia of unity and continuity in Martí's visual and political image and, on the other, reveal themselves as multifaceted discourses that respond to varied and often contradictory ideological and political positions. Obviously each subject participates in collective memories in different registers, and here lies the possible differences between the collective and the individual. But from a theoretical perspective, national discourses open up onto collective memory, which is fed and constituted by individual memories and texts (written, spoken, or visual). And although the collective memory of Cuban society members—or of any other group—is not the same as the memory of any given individual of that community, there are always many basic common elements between the two and its process implies multiple and constant connections.

My analysis then alternates between collective and individual memory, and between certain historical details and their possible relationship to their effects in personal memory. In the end, the fact that the personal contains a great deal of the political (and vice versa) cannot be ignored; politics is always linked to embodied subjects and therefore to personal memory. So an analysis that begins with individual memories, no matter how personal, can still maintain a certain critical validity: the possibility for critique emerges from this diversity and from this stratification. This complex process of simultaneous approaching and distancing can achieve a critical analysis and perhaps outlines the possibility of political agency. Actually, this process, which is both personal and social, lends intensity and creative force to the analysis, and it is exactly here where one finds the possibility of radically questioning the purely political and of suggesting a space from which to rethink and resignify Martí.

I have concentrated on visual culture—photographs, monuments, memorials, statues, paintings, drawings, and movies—because, in addition to my longtime passion for studying Martí's icons, what has been addressed the least in the vast bibliography on

Martí is precisely the effect that these artifacts have had and continue to have on the memory of Cuban citizens and those directly influenced by that "national narrative." All these icons form a fabric of common memories, but I certainly do not imply that all members of this group possess identical recollections. It makes a great deal of sense, then, to examine, for example, both monuments and the rituals of commemoration that are celebrated around them, since those rituals are efforts—always failed ones—to impose a univocal meaning even when it is quite obvious that they are deployed by diverse and even opposing groups and objectives. What these rituals really accomplish is to superimpose multiple meanings that accumulate in a kind of palimpsest and whose contradictions and excesses allow the critic to enter into their gaps and open a space that invites new ways of seeing these icons.

Visual representation conveys the distinction between that which is visualized—and therefore the objectification of the physical and corporeal world—and the immaterial reason of official discourse that wishes to make it succumb. Official state explanations try to tame and control the image, but the image is always heterogeneous and polyvalent. This is why I believe it is possible to use the visual image to destabilize the rigidity of traditionalist discourses, because it always entails an element of otherness and therefore can become a site for contestation. National iconographies, when establishing and hardening themselves in such a way as to turn their referent into a rigid stereotype, make the state viable as the central moment of interpellation, but at the same time these same visual images, viewed critically, retain part of that payload of otherness from which they are derived. My book then does not attempt to establish a visual philology dedicated to rescuing forgotten objects or contents, but instead tries to think of these images more like deposits and instruments of power than as representations of cultural history and "national heritage."

Every national icon, just like every form of embodiment, is always enveloped in a constant slippage of meanings, and this constitutive incompleteness that envelops these icons allows and even invites one to either reaffirm politically convenient meanings or question the signifying solidity that has been presented to us as the national common sense, as its hegemony in the Gramscian sense. This instability of signifying power is precisely where the critic can open possibilities and labor to prevent any particular political or cultural agenda from becoming naturalized or (conversely) demand a false univocality from something that by its very nature requires an interminable opening. I insist, therefore, that contributing to this opening is this book's main goal, as it questions the effects of a hegemonic common sense and thus allows a greater possibility for political and cultural agency. The same Martí iconography that has been used to shore up hegemonic reason can also be used as counterimages and anti-icons. This becomes more feasible in a postmodern era that questions narratives of foundation and origin and even the idea of a national essence.

As Walter Benjamin proposed, I hope to incorporate and develop out of Martí's circulating images a critical strategy opening and rescuing the contingencies enclosed in these representations. I want to identify potential hidden interpretations that can resignify Martí's iconography. Nationalist discourse has been designed like a map of the idealized body of the citizen with the objective to capture the bodies of citizens in order to achieve a high degree of control over their behaviors. Monuments to Martí are erected on the pretext of remembering the hero, but what they really do is monumentalize him in the service of national amnesia, trying to hide their contradictions and everything else that lies outside the hegemonic ideology of the moment. The hero is monumentalized not in order to broaden critical discussion and analysis but to instill reverence and submission to power as represented by a rigid stone image that leads to idolatry.

My work on Martí does not propose to rescue the silenced memories of a specific oppressed group (which was part of the goal of my book *Gay Cuban Nation*) but rather to question Martí's iconolatry in general. This questioning perhaps points to a global need to discern a present and a future that do not completely accord with a traditional understanding of modern nationalisms, in this particular case, Cuban nationalism. From my point of view, an analysis of Martí's visual representations can contribute to the project of undoing a totalizing and homogenous national universe. Hence the conflict between the mythical and the critical: if myth generates a blind faith in a holistic vision of history, critical analysis proposes to allow, via its deconstructive process, the progress of new historical possibilities that work to overcome the national trauma that mentally limits us. A critical approach might create a political agency for the subject who belongs to a collective, hegemonic memory and who should be able to situate herself in some affirmative manner in the globalized world in which we live. What I have tried to achieve in this book is not to preserve what Pierre Nora calls "a restoration of the past" (1989, 7–25) but to feed a desire to orient ourselves in an ever-changing present and thus contribute to the creation of a symbolic map to an unknown future. To achieve this goal one has to place oneself as if in a different world and think differently, questioning that which is most dear and deeply rooted in our hearts (as Martí is for millions, including myself), and from there attempt a new understanding of ourselves as citizens of a rapidly changing world.

NOTES

INTRODUCTION

1. For an extraordinary study of Che Guevara's iconography, see David Kunzle, *Che Guevara*.

2. For some of the innumerable publications on Martí's life and work see Alejandro de la Fuente, *A Nation for All*; Roberto Fernández Retamar, *Introducción a José Martí*; Mauricio Font and Alfonso Quiroz, *The Cuban Republic and José Martí*; Anne Fountain, *José Martí and U.S. Writers*; John Kirk, *José Martí*; Jorge Mañach, *Martí el apóstol*; Lourdes Martínez-Echazábal, "'Martí and the Race'"; Nancy Raquel Mirabal, "'Más que negro'"; Oscar Montero, *José Martí*; *Cuba*; Carlos Ripoll, *La vida íntima y secreta de José Martí*; Julio Rodríguez-Luis, *Re-reading José Martí*; Rafael Rojas, *José Martí*; Cintio Vitier and Fina García Marruz, *Temas martianos*.

3. For two excellent and concise English introductions to Martí's life and work, see Roberto González Echevarría, "José Martí," and Montero, *José Martí*.

4. I use the term *retrospective reconstruction* as an adaptation of the Freudian concept of *Nachträglichkeit* in the sense that it provides the memory, not the event, with traumatic significance and signifies a circular complementarity of both directions of time. It implies a complex and reciprocal relationship between a significant event and its later reinvestment with meaning, a reinvestment that lends it a new psychic efficacy. Translated into French as *après-coup* and into English as "deferred action," *Nachträglichkeit* emphasizes the two traumatic memory vectors: retroactivity and aftereffect. See especially Freud, *The Origins of Psycho-Analysis*; and Lacan, "The Function and Field of Speech and Language in Psychoanalysis."

5. Roland Barthes states, "Not only is the Photograph never, in essence, a memory [. . .] but it actually blocks memory, quickly becomes a counter-memory [. . .]. The photograph is violent: not because it shows violent things, but because on each occasion it fills the sight by force, and because in it nothing can be refused or transformed" (Barthes 1980, 91).

6. Jens Andermann and William Rowe, in the introduction to *Images of Power*, explain that the theoreticians of the Warburg School, despite their ideological differences from Walter Benjamin and the Frankfurt School, coincide with them in the following idea: "Art itself emerges from a region where expression is conceived as unmediated, while the body, on the other hand, is the bearer of a physiological memory that is always already metaphorical" (Andermann and Rowe 2005, 4).

7. Noble's work refers specifically to the Mexican Revolution photographs.

8. Noble says the following about the photograph *Villa en la silla* (Villa on the Seat), implying that a similar phenomenon happens with every national iconic image: "To repeat, after all, is to memorize. Moreover, at the level of address, it must be stressed that this iconic image defies the linear logic of cause and effect that defines historical time. Rather the image is governed by another temporal modality, a modality that belongs to another disciplinary register: namely the psychoanalytical concept *Nachträglichkeit*" (Noble 2005, 209). For the foundation of this study, it is also useful to recall Susannah Radstone's work on the type of relation that results from the historical process and memory: "In place of the quest for the truth of an event, and the history of its causes, *Nachträglichkeit* proposes, rather, that the analysis of memory's tropes can reveal not the truth of the past, but a particular revision prompted by a later event, this pitting psychical contingency against historical truth" (Radstone 2000a, 86).

9. W. J. T. Mitchell explains the distrust and even fear of visual representation underlining Western philosophical thought: "Any attempt to grasp 'the idea of imagery' is fated to wrestle

with the problem of recursive thinking, for the very idea of an 'idea' is bound up with the notion of imagery. 'Idea' comes from the Greek verb 'to see,' and is frequently linked with the notion of the 'eilodon,' the 'visible image' that is fundamental to ancient optics and theories of perception. A sensible way to avoid the temptation of thinking about images in terms of images would be to replace the word 'idea' in discussions of imagery with some term like 'concept' or 'notion,' or to stipulate at the outset that the term 'idea' is to be understood as something quite different from imagery or pictures. This is a strategy of the Platonic tradition, which distinguishes the eidos from the eidolon by conceiving of the former as a 'suprasensible reality' of 'forms, types, or species,' the latter as a sensible impression that provides a mere 'likeness' (eikon) or 'semblance' (phantasma) of the eidos" (Mitchell 1986, 5–6). Elaborating on Mitchell's contention, Andermann and Rowe state that "it is in this spectral substantiality, precisely, that the image tends to return as the repressed other of language—and of written language in particular—which has supposedly exorcised it but in whose very substance it re-emerges in manifold forms of tropes, figures of speech, calligraphies and cryptographies. As in all antagonisms, then, in the contest between images and ideas, each of the contenders is from the very outset affected and contaminated by that which it constitutes as its other" (Andermann and Rowe 2005, 1).

10. Christian Metz explains Barthes concept of *punctum*, writing, "For Barthes, the only part of a photograph which entails the feeling of an off-frame space is what he calls the *punctum*, the point of sudden and strong emotion, of small trauma, it can be a tiny detail" (Metz 1990, 161). Metz's explanation strongly implies a connection between Barthes's concept of the *punctum* and Benjamin's *aura* and *reciprocal gaze*, as well as Freud's and Lacan's *fetish*, *mourning*, and *Nachträglichkeit* (see note 4 of this chapter for on *retrospective reconstruction* as an adaptation of Freud's and Lacan's *Nachträglichkeit*). The *punctum* is the point of strong emotion in a photograph that

produces the feeling of an off frame. This is related to the foundation of Freud's *fetish* and *mourning*: these emotions constitute a central part of the memory process of the retrospective reconstruction (*Nachträglichkeit*) that constructs a discourse based, not on a past event, but on the person's feelings about a past traumatic experience. Benjamin's reciprocal gaze, the emotional exchange between the observer and the observed, centers mainly on the *punctum* of the image and incites a form of individual and even magical feeling that Benjamin relates to a residue of what he calls the aura of the work of art.

11. I am referring here, of course, to Ángel Rama's groundbreaking study *The Lettered City* in which this Latin American theorist shows the power of the written discourse in the formation and maintenance of Latin American societies since colonial times and the crucial role that cities play in displaying and applying power. To impose order on a vast New World empire, the Iberian monarchs created carefully planned cities where institutional and legal powers were administered through a specialized cadre of elite men called *letrados*; it is the urban nexus of lettered culture and state power that Rama calls "the lettered city." Starting with the colonial period, Rama undertakes a historical analysis of the hegemonic influences of the written word. He explores the place of writing and urbanization in the imperial designs of the Iberian colonialists and views the city both as a rational order of signs representative of the Enlightenment progress and as the site where the Old World is transformed—according to detailed written instructions—in the New World. His analysis continues by recounting the social and political challenges faced by the letrados as their roles in society widened to include those of journalist, fiction writer, essayist, and political leader, and how those roles changed through the independence movements of the nineteenth century. The coming of the twentieth century, and especially the gradual emergence of a mass reading public, brought further challenges. Through a discussion

of the currents and countercurrents in the turn-of-the-century literary life, Rama shows how the city of letters was finally "revolutionized" (Rama 1996). As it has already been studied by so many scholars and commentators in our time, the power of the written discourse under the control of the lettered men in colonial Latin America articulated by Rama has been largely substituted by much more dispersed, impersonal, and globalized entities with the advent of what can be called the visual era in the twentieth and twenty-first centuries (see García Canclini 1989; Martín-Barbero 1987).

12. An excellent collection of articles on the Special Period can be found in Ariana Hernandez-Reguant, *Cuba in the Special Period.*

CHAPTER 1

1. George Washington Halsey's Havana gallery was located at 26 Obispo Street. The first Cuban to own a daguerreotype studio in Havana was Esteban de Arteaga, who in 1843 acquired a gallery located at 71 Lamparilla Street (Del Valle 2004, 2). The original news about the historic opening of Halsey's business was published in the Havana newspaper *El Noticioso y Lucero* on January 3, 1941. For more information, see Oller Oller 2010, 1; Oller Oller 2010, 2; and Oller Oller 1843, 4.

2. This is the title given by Martí to one of his articles published in Caracas: "¡Los fotógrafos poblarán el mundo!," *La Opinión Nacional,* January 1885.

3. "Progreso inmenso fue el conseguir fijar las imágenes obtenidas en la cámara oscura, pero no es menos cierto que el hombre no se ha manifestado satisfecho con todos los adelantos realizados por la fotografía. Cerca de medio siglo hace que se está buscando con empeño el conseguir fijar también los colores, o sea obtener las imágenes con su coloración propia. Este gran invento, repetidas veces anunciado como conseguido, pero nunca realizado, parece al fin resuelto por un procedimiento ideado por M. M. Cros y Carpentier, quienes

acaban de presentar a la Academia de Ciencias de París fotografías de una acuarela, en las que se notan exactamente repro-
ducidos los detalles y colores del original. En fotografías se
han sacado por medio de tres clisés para cada objeto; clisés
obtenidos respectivamente a través de tres diafragmas líqui-
dos, uno anaranjado, otro verde y otro violeta. La opacidad
y la transparencia varían de un clisé a otro en las porciones
homólogas de la imagen, a fin de distribuir las cantidades
relativas del rojo, amarillo y azul (que son los colores simples
que forman todos los de la naturaleza), de manera que com-
pongan y reproduzcan todos los matices del modelo. La capa
de colodión sensible fijada sobre el papel o sobre el vidrio,
para obtener las pruebas negativas, se empapa en bicromato de
amoníaco y después se seca en la estufa. [. . .] Por este medio
es fácil obtener imágenes fotográficas de toda clase de colores.
Para ello es necesario repetir tres veces la operación sobre un
mismo vidrio, empleando para la imagen obtenida a través del
diafragma verde un baño colorante rojo: para la imagen del
diafragma anaranjado un baño verde, y por último, para el
diafragma violeta, baño amarillo. Será verdaderamente mágico
conseguir fotografías, en que a la exacta copia de la naturaleza
en cuanto a las líneas, se consiga unir la viveza y animación
del colorido." (The original of this article appeared in Caracas
in *La Opinión Nacional*, December 2, 1881. I take this quo-
tation from Martí 1975a, 103–4. See also Bermúdez 1990,
92–94. In his article, Bermúdez comments not only on the
aforementioned text but also on two other of Martí's articles
about photography, including "Una fotografía en un revólver"
[1884] and "¡Los fotógrafos poblarán el mundo!" [1885].)

4. "¡Ruines tiempos, en que no priva más arte que el de llenar
bien los graneros de la casa, y sentarse en silla de oro, y vivir
todo dorado; sin ver que la naturaleza humana no ha de cam-
biar de cómo es, y con sacar el oro afuera, no se hace sino
quedarse sin oro alguno adentro! ¡Ruines tiempos, en que son
mérito eximio y desusado el amor y el ejercicio de la grandeza!
[. . .] ¡Ruines tiempos, en que los sacerdotes no merecen ya

la alabanza ni la veneración de los poetas, ni los poetas han comenzado todavía a ser sacerdotes! [. . .].ˮ (Martí 1975c, 223–24). *Poema del Niágara* was written by Venezuelan poet Juan Antonio Pérez Bonalde and was later reproduced in *Revista de Cuba* in 1883 (see Martí 1975c, 7, 221–38). The English translation comes from Esther Allen (Martí 2002, 43–44).

5. "Todo es expansión, comunicación, florescencia, contagio, esparcimiento. [. . .] Ni la originalidad literaria cabe, ni la libertad política subsiste mientras no se asegure la libertad espiritual. El primer trabajo del hombre es reconquistarse. [. . .] Sólo lo genuino es fructífero. Sólo lo directo es poderoso. [. . .]" (Martí 1975c, 7, 225–30; Martí 2002, 46–49).

6. There is a long-standing fierce polemic between those who propose a close relationship between Marxism and Martí's social positions and those who reject such relationship. The polemic has a clear and intense political overtone, and it is not my intention here to inject myself in this debate. Instead, I aim here to trace the similarities and differences between Marxism and Martí's position on the new modern technologies (in particular photography) that were emerging in the second half of the nineteenth century. Among the many works supporting strong affinities between Marxism and Martí's position, see Armando Hart Dávalos, "Martí y Marx"; Juan Marinello, "El caso literario de José Martí"; Roberto Fernández Retamar, "Martí, Lenin y la revolución anticolonial"; and Julio Antonio Mella, "Glosas al pensamiento de José Martí." A contrasting position can be found in Carlos Ripoll, "The Falsification of José Martí in Cuba" and *José Martí, the United States, and the Marxist Interpretation of Cuban History*; Enrico Mario Santí, "José Martí and the Cuban Revolution"; Rafael Rojas, "Otro gallo cantaría" and in his *Motivos de Anteo*, 143–64; and Bruno Bosteels, "Marx y Martí."

7. "Primer retrato conocido de Martí, de su época de escolar. Se supone que la medallita corresponde a un premio de Sobresaliente en las clases de Inglés en el colegio 'San Anacleto,' de

Rafael Sixto Casado. Existe una copia de esta fotografía en la Biblioteca Nacional 'José Martí,' en La Habana, entregada el 12 de julio de 1902 a Domingo Figarola-Caneda, primer director de la Biblioteca, por el peluquero Enrique Bermúdez. Martí, de muchacho, acompañaba frecuentemente a Bermúdez cuando éste iba a trabajar a los teatros, para poder asistir tras bambalinas a las funciones. Otra copia fue enviada por la madre de Martí, doña Leonor Pérez, a Marcelina de Aguirre, madrina de bautismo del niño, quien escribió al dorso: *José Martí nació en la Habana, fue su madrina Da. Marcelina de Aguirre.* Tiene, además, impresa una corona entre dos ramas de laurel y la leyenda: *E. Mestre—Fotógrafo con Real Privilege— O'Reilly 63—Habana*" (Quesada y Miranda 1985, 8).

8. Regarding this issue, Barthes says that "The photography is violent: not because it shows violent things but because on each occasion it fills the sight by force" (Barthes 1980, 91).

9. Benjamin describes the nineteenth century as "the period of those studios—with their draperies and palm trees, their tapestries and easels—which occupied so ambiguous a place between execution and representation, between torture chamber and throne room, and of which an early portrait of Kafka brings us a deeply moving [*erschütternd*] testimony. There the boy stands, perhaps six years old, dressed up in a humiliatingly tight children's suit overloaded with trimming, in a sort of greenhouse landscape. The background is thick with palm fronds. And as if to make these upholstered tropics even stuffier and more oppressive, the subject holds in his left hand an inordinately large broad-brimmed hat, such as Spaniards wear. He would surely disappear in this setting were it not for his immeasurably sad eyes, which reign over this landscape predestined for them. This picture, in its boundless sadness, forms a pendant to the early photographs in which people did not yet look out at the world in so excluded and godforsaken a manner as this boy. There was an aura about them, a medium that lent fullness and security to their gaze as it penetrated that medium" (Benjamin, 1999b, 515–16). Carolin

Duttlinger explains that "[w]ithin Benjamin's writings, [. . .] aura and photography are not simply cast as mutually exclusive opposites but are in fact engaged in a complex process of interaction" (2008, 80). The complexity of the aura effect starting at the end of the nineteenth century is symptomatic of a general change in human perception and experience—that is, it "reflects a wider condition of modernity: the turn toward seriality and uniformity which shapes the experience of reality, in particular in the modern city" (2008, 82). Then, from these ideas about the general relationship between modernity, seriality, and uniformity in Martí's time, we can better understand the cause of the tension between what was happening in the modernizing world of Martí and his ideas regarding art and society. If his insistence on authenticity and originality was in contradiction to the seriality and uniformity that was invading every aspect of human production at that time; and if photography was one of those modern phenomena mechanically reproducing images, including those of the human body, then we have to conclude that Martí's position toward photography had to be paradoxical. But then how do we explain his obvious fascination with photography and his interest on his own photographic image? The problem is rather complex. On the one hand, Martí participated, as we have seen, in the enthusiasm for the new invention of photography, and used it—especially but not exclusively in the bust portraits of the last four years of his life—in favor of his political and moral ideas. But on the other, we have to find an explanation for the manner in which he adapted his ideas about art and society to his participation in the new invention. For this we can return to some of Benjamin's meditations; remember he said that "in the fleeting expression of the human face, the aura beckons from early photographs for the last time" (Benjamin 1969b, 226). In other words, photography appears here "not only as the tool of aura's destruction but also in the form of the early photographic portrait, as the site of its last appearance" (Duttlinger 2008, 83).

10. "Retrato de Martí, seguramente hecho en Madrid durante la primera deportación. Apareció publicado en una hoja suelta distribuida por el periódico *Cuba*, de Tampa, en 1895, al anunicar la llegada de Martí a tierra cubana, y por el periódico *El Fígaro*, de La Habana, el 26 de mayo de 1895, al comunicar la noticia de la muerte del Apóstol" (Quesada y Miranda 1985, 18).

11. "Retrato de Martí en traje de presidiario, al ser condenado a seis años de prisión por infidencia. Dedicó una copia a su madre, doña Leonor Pérez, escribiendo debajo: *1 Brigada—113*; y al dorso: *Mírame, madre, y por tu amor no llores: / Si esclavo de mi edad y mis doctrinas, / Tu mártir corazón llené de espinas, / Piensa que nacen entre espinas flores. José Martí Presidio, 28 de Agosto de 1870*. Envió otra copia a Fermín Valdés Domínguez, preso en La Cabaña, con la dedicatoria: *Hermano de dolor, —no mires nunca / En mí al esclavo que cobarde llora;— / Ve la imagen robusta de mi alma / Y la página bella de mi historia. José Martí Presidio, 28 de Agosto de 1870*" (Quesada y Miranda *Iconografía martiana*, 16).

12. "Mírame, madre, y por tu amor no llores: / Si esclavo de mi edad y mis doctrinas, / Tu mártir corazón llené de espinas, / Piensa que nacen entre espinas flores. José Martí" (Quesada y Miranda 1985, 16).

13. "Hermano de dolor, —no mires nunca / En mí al esclavo que cobarde llora;— / Ve la imagen robusta de mi alma / Y la página bella de mi historia. José Martí." (Quesada y Miranda 1985, 16).

14. Ottmar Ette takes this image from Martínez Estrada (1967, 16–17). There are many variations of the manipulated image of Martí in prison (Ette 1994, 266). Quesada y Miranda gives the following information about this photo: "Apareció publicado en una hoja suelta distribuida por el periódico *Cuba*, de Tampa, en 1895, al anunicar la llegada de Martí a tierra cubana, y por el periódico *El Fígaro*, de La Habana, el 26 de mayo de 1895, al comunicar la noticia de la muerte del Apóstol [. . .] It appeared [together with the photo of Figure 1.2]

on a flyer distributed by the newspaper *Cuba*, of Tampa, Florida, in 1895, in order to announce Martí's arrival on Cuban soil, and by the newspaper *El Fígaro*, of Havana, on May 26, 1895, when the news of the Apostle's death was published" (Quesada y Miranda 1985, 18).

15. For an insightful study of Martí's efforts to distancing himself from the so-called modernist decadence, see Sylvia Molloy, "Too Wilde for Comfort."

16. "Debe señalarse, entre las más recientes [estatuas], *Preso 113*, concebida por José Villa a partir de la foto que se le tomara a Martí en la cárcel, en 1870. Erigida en la Fragua Martiana, donde aún quedan restos de lo que fueran las canteras de San Lázaro, acusa una de las características que mejor particulariza las esculturas de este autor: su resignificación a partir de ubicarlas en contextos reales" (Bermúdez 1999, 23).

17. The original of this poetry collection was published in New York by Lovis Weiss in 1891.

18. "Retrato de Martí tomado el 10 de octubre de 1892, en Kingston, Jamaica, por el patriota y fotógrafo Juan Bautista Valdés. Hay una copia con la siguiente dedicación: *Al hijo eminente de Cuba, que la defiende de sus peligros y la honra con su vida creadora, a mi amigo abnegado y viril José Mayner, su José Martí Kinston, 13 de Ocbre. 1892.* Esta copia tiene impresa en relieve la firma del fotógrafo y la leyenda: *J. B. Valdés.—Studio—85 Kenn Street—Kingston.* Existe otra copia dedicada por Martí a Esteban Borrero: *A su herm o Esteban. Pepe New York*" (Quesada y Miranda 1985, 31).

19. "Retrato de Martí hecho en Washington, según el patriota puertorriqueño Sotero Figueroa, por los días en que sesionaba la Comisión Monetaria Internacional Americana, en la que Martí representaba a la República de Uruguay. Figueroa y Gonzalo de Quesada y Aróstegui aseguraban que a Martí no le agradaba este retrato pues consideraba petulante la posición escogida por el fotógrafo" (Quesada y Miranda 1985, 44).

20. "Autorretrato de Martí. El original sólo mide dos centímetros de alto. En la misma hoja hay otros dibujos suyos y la frase

Por América, repetida varias veces" (Quesada y Miranda 1985, 112).

21. "Martí con su hijo José Francisco. Esta zincografía fue hecha seguramente en la ciudad de La Habana" (Quesada y Miranda 1985, 30).

22. As I said before, Martí's modernista stance was paradoxical in the sense that he was trying to balance his position in favor of, on one hand, art for art's sake, and on the other, a political art in conjunction to his very active political life.

23. For an interesting and pertinent study of the implications of the daguerreotype in the nineteenth century, see Susan S. Williams, "'The Inconstant Daguerreotype.'"

CHAPTER 2

1. For an informative and thoughtful discussion of national sites in general and Latin American monuments in particular, see Elizabeth Jelin, *Los trabajos de la memoria*.

2. José Villalta Saavedra studied in the Colegio San Carlos and later moved to the City of Cienfuegos, entering the workshop of the marble mason and sculptor Miguel Valls. Later he moved to Florence, where he continued his studies at the Academy of Fine Arts. He became known in Cuba when he won first place in the competition to design a monument for the medical students executed in 1871. He used his winnings and sold his possessions in order to pay the price of building the monument to Martí in Havana's Central Park. Sick and unable to support himself, he returned to Italy, his second homeland, and died in Rome. In the exhibition that took place in 1940 at the University of Havana, called "300 Years of Art in Cuba," two of his works were displayed (Galería Cubarte n.d., "José Villlalta Saavedra").

3. Mario Santí (1911–88) is the sculptor of this mausoleum. "He completed primary school in his native city and secondary school in Santiago de Cuba. In 1928, he was awarded a scholarship by Oriente Province to study in Havana. He entered

the San Alejandro Art Academy wherein 1934 he earned the title of Professor of Drawing and Painting and Drawing and Modelling. Some of his numerous prizes are 1945 First Prize in the National Competition for his Monument to Mothers in the City of Cárdenas and 1945 First Prize for the Construction of a Dignified Tomb for Martí the Apostle in the Cemetery of Santiago de Cuba. He also created works like the bust of General Maceo in Holguín, Oriente; the Pantheon of Veterans in Bayamo; the Statue of José Martí and six colossal statues symbolizing the six provinces of Cuba, the Primitive Sculptor at the National University, many busts in different cities, public and private collections in Cuba and abroad" (Galería Cubarte. n.d., "Mario Santí").

4. For an insightful discussion of Peirce's concept of *index* and its significance in film studies, see Mary Ann Doane, "The Indexical and the Concept of Medium Specificity."

5. Another version of this article was published in Enrico Mario Santí, *Pensar a José Martí*, 1–9. The English expanded version of this article is "Thinking through Martí."

6. I thank my doctoral student Jonathan Dettman for suggesting to me the idea that the Fragua Martiana is probably the most shrine-like of Havana's Martí sites. Dettman, who visited Havana on the summer of 2011 as part of his research, is finishing his dissertation, tentatively titled "Writing after History."

7. This work was designed by Juan José Sicre (1898–1974), founder of Cuba's avant-garde sculpture. His academic background began in the Vallate Academy and continued in the San Alejandro Art Academy. Between 1920 and 1922 he studied at the Royal Academy of San Fernando in Madrid and then moved to Paris, where he studied at the Grande Chaumière. In 1926, Sicre had his first personal showing for the Societé Paris-Amerique Latine. Starting in 1927 he held a full professorship at San Alejandro, which he held throughout the 1930s. Later he received an award from the National Exposition of Painting and Sculpture, a prize in the International

Competition for the Monument to Martí and first prize in the International Competition to build a monument to Eugenio María de Hostos, in the Dominican Republic. In 1940, he displayed his personal work at the University of Havana. Sicre took part in the important exposition "300 Years of Art in Cuba." Among the many environmental works that he bequeathed to the national artistic heritage, the monument to José Martí in the Civic Plaza of Havana (now Revolution Plaza) stands out (Galería Cubarte. n.d., "Juan José Sicre").

8. In *Havana*, Joseph Scarpaci, Roberto Segre, and Mario Coyula write the following about Enrique Luis Varela and the controversy that shaped Batista's stylistic decision about Martí's monument at the former Civic Plaza: "Projects concerned with defining central Havana continued [during Batista's government], including works tied to the Plaza Cívica and the Pro-José Martí Central Commission initiated at an Inter-American design competition. Despite difficulty in finding support for the project, the architect Aquiles Maza and the sculptor Juan José Sicre won the design competition in 1942" (2002, 74–75). A few pages further in the same book, they write, "The decision of the government of Fulgencio Batista to build the José Martí Monument in the Plaza Cívica in Havana generated bitter controversy. Personal and political motives made Batista award the design to the [. . .] team headed by Enrique Luis Varela [. . .] Its design was exhibited and provoked heated discussion in a forum organized by the Institute of Architects (Colegio de Arquitectos), the principal professional organization of Cuban architects" (81).

9. "At least three problems—design, semiotics, and contract biding—plagued the Plaza Cívica project from the outset. The Palacio de Justicia (Justice Palace; José Pérez Benitoa, architect; 1957), a prominent element in the plan, was a structure of mastodonic proportions. Transformed in the late 1960s as the Palacio de la Revolución, it looked like a Creole rendition of a classic-modern Mussolinesque building in L'EUR 42 (Esposizione Universale di Roma, 1942). At its side stood the

lamentable monument to Cuba's national hero, José Martí. Ironically, the obelisk from the Martí Monument was a copy of a Schenley Whiskey advertisement that appeared in the 1939 World's Fair of New York" (Scarpaci, Segre, and Coyula 2002, 128).

10. For information about Batista's decision regarding the obelisk and statue at the Civic Plaza, see Scarpaci, Segre, and Coyula, *Havana*.

11. Jay Winter says the following about the relationship between sites of memory and historical meaning: "Sites of memory are places where people affirm their faith that history has a meaning. What kind of site is appropriate where the majority of people see no meaning at all in the events being marked in time and place? Ignoring Auschwitz or Hiroshima is impossible, but locating them within earlier commemorative structures or gestures is either problematic or absurd or both" (2010, 322).

12. In what follows, Winter explains some of the reasons for the preference of obelisks as sites of memory in modern times: "By the later decades of the twentieth century, artistic opinion and aesthetic tastes had changed sufficiently to make abstraction the key language of commemorative expression" (2010, 321). In the same article he refers specifically to the modern use of the obelisk in national monuments: "In Protestant countries, the aesthetic debate took on a quasi-religious character. War memorials with crosses on them offended some Protestants, who believed that the Reformation of the sixteenth century precluded such 'Catholic' notation. Obelisks were preferable, and relatively inexpensive too. In France, war memorials were by law restricted to public and not church grounds, though many local groups found a way around this prescription" (2010, 320). Although Cuba has never been a Protestant country, Winter offers a helpful explanation of the modern artistic tendency toward abstraction versus sacred figures in the construction of national monuments even when, like in Martí's memory, the honored hero is revered like a secular saint.

13. Anna Hyatt Huntington (1876–1973), the sculptor of the equestrian Martí in New York Central Park, was especially well known for her works of animals, which perhaps explains why she preferred to sculpt Martí on horseback. Huntington was born in Cambridge, Massachusetts. Her father, Alpheus Hyatt, was a professor of paleontology and zoology at Harvard University and Massachusetts Institute of Technology and served as a contributing factor to her early interest in animals and animal anatomy. In addition to her formal studies, she spent many hours doing extensive study of animals in zoos and circuses. She married Archer Milton Huntington, and because of her husband's enormous wealth and the shared interests of the couple, the Huntingtons were responsible for founding 14 museums and 4 wildlife preserves (Bronze Gallery. n.d., "Anna Hyatt"; Whyld 2005).

14. Although I have not dealt with it in this book, it is worth mentioning that Miami and South Florida have witnessed similar ideological self-legitimization with the use of Martí's iconography by a variety of political groups among the exiled Cuban community. João Felipe Gonçalves has recently worked on this issue (see Gonçalves 2007 and Gonçalves 2010).

15. These are some of the titles of *New York Times* articles published during that period: "Central Park Ceremony for Cuban Hero Erupts Into Riot Over Castro," "Disputed Statue of Cuban To Go Up: City Will Put Jose Marti Figure in Central Park After 13-Year Wait," "Statue of Cuban Hero Out in Open," "Statue of Cuban Finally Placed," "City Unveils Statue of Marti on Tuesday," and "Cubans Fail in Attempt to place Martí Statue: Exiles Find Plater Model Too Heavy to Lift to Pedestal."

16. This sculpture was made by the Cuban artist Andrés González González (Pinar del Río, 1957). González studied in the National School of Art and graduated in Monumental Sculpture from the Surikov Superior Institute of Art (Moscow) in 1986. After returning from the Soviet Union, Andrés began to work on the Nation Commission for the Development of

Monumental and Environmental Sculpture (CODEMA). He is the sculptor of well-known monuments in Cuba and abroad, one of which is the God Neptune, in front of the eponymously name hotel in Havana (1991). He sculpted the José Martí that presides over the Anti-Imperialist Tribune on Havana's Malecón. Also of interest to this study are the following comments in "Noticias de Arquitectura" about this statue: "The statue of José Martí [. . .] is a new version of the independence hero: a burly Martí, with large pectorals and thick legs, holding a child [Elian?], standing up manfully to the enemy and, with his left arm extended, pointing accusingly, perhaps, towards the empire, in this case the United States Interests Office. According to the sculptor himself, the idea is of an accusing and protective Martí, holding childhood in his arms, like the future of humanity, and the physical strength of the monument isn't a gratuitous act, but rather symbolizes the strength of Cubans' ideas" (n.d., "Andrés González González").

17. Concerning the "nature" of sites of memory (including, of course, monuments) and their actuality and contemporary social and political force, Winter says the following: "Anyone who even glances at all the power of living sites of memory in Latin America or India, for example, will realize that the distinction [Pierre Nora's distinction between authentic *milieux de mémoire* being occupied by inauthentic *lieux de mémoire*] cannot hold. *Milieux de mémoire* are alive and well, and so are oral and written traditions of remembrance that inform them" (2010, 315; see also Nora 1989). My take on this is that there is no distinction between authentic and inauthentic sites because they are all sites of memory constructed by visual, oral, and written traditions. It is not that *lieux* sites take over *milieux* ones, but that there is a palimpsestic layering of different types of sites of memory, and none are authentic or inauthentic. Also, although I agree with Winter's idea about the power that sites of memory still have in some societies, I argue that that power might be reaching a moment in which a

globalized culture opens up a fundamental line of questioning that eventually will weaken the political effectiveness of those sites.

18. There is a long-standing fierce polemic between those who propose a close relationship between Marxism and Martí's social positions and those who reject such relationship. (For more information about this issue, see Chapter 1, note 15.)

CHAPTER 3

1. My translation.
2. The concept of the *reciprocal gaze* is my adaptation of the *imaginary encounter* developed by Carolin Duttlinger in her article "Imaginary Encounters."
3. For a study of the indexical sign in photography and film, see Doane, "The Indexical and the Concept of Medium Specificity." Charles Sanders Peirce explains his concepts of index, icon, and symbol in many of his writings, in this occasion I have used Peirce, *Writings of Charles S. Peirce*, 1: 475–76, 485–86. For other excellent discussions on the practical and ontological consequences produced by the digital cinema and its impact on the photographic origins of the celluloid film, see Garrett Stewart, *Framed Time*, and Cathy Hannabach's "Photographic Traces and Cinematic Returns." On the technical questions of *José Martí: The Eye of the Canary*, I have to clarify that Fernando Pérez, in an electronic correspondence on January 23, 2012, explained to me that the movie was filmed in high-resolution digital and then converted to a negative cinematographic film. He also said that at the present time there are some copies of the film in 35 mm, and others in different digital versions (Blu-ray Disc, etc).
4. Quesada y Miranda offers the following about this image: "Primer retrato conocido de Martí, de su época de escolar. Se supone que la medallita corresponde a un premio de Sobresaliente en las clases de Inglés en el colegio 'San Anacleto,' de Rafael Sixto Casado. Existe una copia de esta fotografía en

la Biblioteca Nacional 'José Martí,' en La Habana, entregada el 12 de julio de 1902 a Domingo Figarola-Caneda, primer director de la Biblioteca, por el peluquero Enrique Bermúdez. Martí, de muchacho, acompañaba frecuentemente a Bermúdez cuando éste iba a trabajar a los teatros, para poder asistir tras bambalinas a las funciones. Otra copia fue enviada por la madre de Martí, doña Leonor Pérez, a Marcelina de Aguirre, madrina de bautismo del niño, quien escribió al dorso: *José Martí nació en la Habana, fue su madrina Da. Marcelina de Aguirre.* Tiene, además, impresa una corona entre dos ramos de laurel y la leyenda: E. Mestre—Fotógrafo con Real Privilegio—O'Reilly 63—Habana" ("First known portrait of Martí, from his school years. It is thought that the little medal is for an 'Outstanding' recognition in English at Rafael Sixto Casado's 'San Anacleto' school. There is a copy of this photograph in the José Martí National Library, in Havana, donated to the library's first director, Domingo Figarola-Caneda, by the hairdresser Enrique Bermúdez. Martí, as a boy, often accompanied Bermúdez when he went to work in the theaters, in order to attend the performances from backstage. Another copy was sent by his mother, Mrs. Leonor Pérez, to Marcelina de Aguirre, the boy's godmother, who wrote on the back: *José Martí born in Havana, his godmother being Da. Marcelina de Aguirre.* It also exhibits a stamp of a crown between laurel branches with the legend: *E. Mestre–Fotógrafo con Real Privilegio–O' Reilly 63–La Habana*"; 1985, 8–9).

5. In spite of the fact that the image of faces in Figure 3.2 and Figure 3.3 are not identical, there is little doubt that these two images have the closest resemblance of the entire film. From the theoretical perspective, this similarity highlights Mary Ann Doane's assertion—elaborating on Peirce's ideas—that both photography and film are sign systems "that merge icon, index, and to some extent, symbol" (Doane 2006, 134).

6. Noble, referring to the *Villa en la silla* (Villa on the Seat) photography, implies that a similar phenomenon occurs with any national iconic image (Noble 2005, 209).

7. Many scholars consider Martí to be the founder of Modernismo, the first truly Hispano-American literary movement (Jrade 1998; Schulman 1966). Modernismo was a complex and contradictory literary and cultural movement that arose in response to modernity's excessive scientism, commercialism, and technological explosion, associated mostly with industrialized countries but that also began to be felt in Latin America. Unlike these modernizing forces, Modernismo highlighted spiritual, poetic, and antibourgeois values. As I said before, Martí attributed great importance to political action and elevated morality, and that made him different, for example, from a so-called "decadent" modernista like Julián del Casal (Jrade 1998; Fernández Retamar 1969). Julio Ramos has done some of the most penetrating research into this captivating topic by questioning the idea (common in Martí scholarship) that Martí was an "organic subject" in the sense that he was able to completely integrate writing and political action. Perhaps Martí's greatest philosophical contribution was to have tried (successfully or not) to achieve an organic relationship between writing and life by way of a heroic will that would overcome the instability of traditional values in modern society. Additionally, in his effort to achieve this goal, Martí proposed the modern poet as critic of the law and as ally of nature. His writing, then, even when obviously political, is always laden with metaphors and symbols so that the poet is always present (Ramos 1989, 7–16, 145–243).

8. For a study of the relationship among photography, fetishes, and mourning, see Christian Metz, "Photography and Fetish." Metz argues that "[f]ilm is [. . .] an extraordinary activator of fetishism" (162) and that "film is more capable of playing on fetishism, photography more capable of itself becoming a fetish" (164).

9. The film reflects the mythification of Martí by encouraging audiences to have intense, emotional, and patriotic reactions to its scenes, inviting them to cry or otherwise perform their nationalist affect. Radstone's analysis of the ideological and psychological function of this phenomenon in *Forrest Gump*

is useful for understanding what is at work in *José Martí: The Eye of the Canary*: "Forrest emerges as both omnipotent and utterly passive. According to psychoanalysis, however, this convergence of passivity and omnipotence is anything but paradoxical, but constitutes, rather, two sides of narcissism's coin. Infantile narcissism is understood by psychoanalysis as a necessary development stage in which the child experiences itself as part of the parent, who is fantasised as all-powerful. This fantasy of omnipotence can then be drawn on to counter a growing awareness of insufficiency, incompleteness and dependency. In adulthood and at times on stress, such fantasies may be re-evoked. According to one commentator on melodrama's characteristic affects and fantasies, the confluence of feelings of powerlessness with fantasies of omnipotence is inextricably linked with melodrama's characteristic orchestrations of temporality and point of view. [. . .] Tears, argues [Steve] Neale, testify to the acknowledgement of powerlessness in the face of the irreversibility of time" (Radstone 2000c, 100).

CHAPTER 4

1. In 1953, the young Fidel Castro stood accused of participating in and leading the failed attack on the Moncada barracks during Fulgencio Batista's government. During the trial, he wrote and delivered his famous statement *La historia me absolverá* (*History Will Absolve Me*) as a form of self-defense. In his statement, Castro declared that José Martí was the intellectual author of his July 26th political movement, which organized the attack. For a reproduction of a photograph of the young Castro in front of a photo of Martí in the background, see Ette 1994, 278.

2. The contrast between the technological and political possibilities of photography in Martí's time and his uncharacteristic refusal to use this medium during his bellicose activities on Cuban soil has been analyzed by Jorge R. Bermúdez, a professor

of Cuban art at the University of Havana, in *Antología visual José Martí*, 14.

3. "La conciencia artística del señor Valderrama es tan severa que además de documentarse cuanto le fue dable, se trasladó a Dos Ríos, alojóse allí y todos sus bocetos fueron hechos a la hora de la trágica caída del Apóstol, colocando el modelo en la posición que los biógrafos declaran que ocupaba Martí y utilizando la luz en la dirección adecuada. Eligió, además, el mes de mayo, no obstante ser de lluvias y propenso a plagas en nuestros campos, y mal alojado, con todas las dificultades del transporte, llevó a cabo su obra sin otra ambición ni estímulo que su gran amor al Maestro y su fervor artístico, sin propósito alguno de lucro" (Carricarte quoted in Bermúdez 2004, 17).

4. "Creada en 1917, representó a Valderrama en el Salón de Bellas Artes de 1918. No obstante, la crítica no le fue favorable, señalándole algunas inexactitudes históricas, que poco o nada le restaban a la obra. Pero fue suficiente para que el amor propio del gran pintor académico la destruyera. En consecuencia, el único testimonio visual a color de la misma, una tricromía que publicara en su cubierta la revista *Bohemia* (24 de febrero de 1918) al coincidir la efemérides del inicio de la Guerra del 1895 y la apertura del mencionado Salón, ha sido la imagen a partir de la cual se ha restaurado digitalmente el lienzo de Valderrama para esta *Antología visual*, luego de ochenta y cinco años de su exposición y posterior destrucción" (Bermúdez 2004, 17).

5. On June 9, 1895, Higinio Martínez's photograph of Martí's head appeared on the front page of the Cuban journal *La Caricatura*. According to the photographer, the photograph was taken on May 27, 1895.

6. "Aunque dicha fotografía está sacada—a los ochos días de muerto [. . .] en el combate de Dos Ríos no obstante los prorgresos de una rápida descomposición a causa de la humedad del terreno, todos han reconocido al revolucionario señor Martí, pues los rasgos distintivos de su fisonomía no han podido en ese tiempo ser borrados por la mano de la muerte.

La frente espaciosa que daba a su rostro un sello tan especial, el cabello rizoso, y otras señales del cuerpo, convienen exactamente con los retratos que todo el mundo conoce y con los antecedentes suministrados por sus familiares, por lo cual el cadáver ha sido debidamente identificado. Al mismo tiempo le remito fotografías del cementerio, el ataúd en que fue conducido Martí desde Remanganaguas y el nicho en que reposa en la Necrópolis" (quoted in Oller Oller 2010a). According to the information provided by Oller Oller, Martínez signed this statement on June 1, 1895, in Santiago de Cuba.

7. There are new interpretations of Martí in essays, but this book focuses on iconography, which is why I restrict my comments to this topic only.

8. For insightful studies of the Freudian idea of mourning and repetition of trauma in a Latin American context, see Avelar, *The Untimely Present*; Masiello, "Scribbling on the Wreck"; and Lazzara, "Pinochet's Cadaver as Ruin and Palimpsest."

BIBLIOGRAPHY

Achúgar, Hugo. 2003. "'El lugar de la memoria, a propósito de monumentos (motivos y paréntesis).'" In *Monumentos, memoriales y marcas
territoriales*, edited by Elizabeth Jelin and Victoria Langland, 191–216.
Madrid and Buenos Aires: Siglo XXI Editores.

Allen, Esther, ed. 2002. *José Martí: Selected Writings*. New York: Penguin
Books.

Andermann, Jens, and William Rowe, eds. 2005. *Images of Power: Iconography, Culture and the State in Latin America*. New York: Berghahn
Books.

Anderson, Benedict. 1983. *Imagined Communities: Reflections on the Origin and Spread of Nationalism*. London: Verso.

Avelar, Idelber. 1999. *The Untimely Present: Postdictatorial Latin American
Fiction and the Task of Mourning*. Durham and London: Duke University Press.

Barthes, Roland. 1980. *Camera Lucida: Reflections on Photography*. Translated by Richard Howard. London: Vintage.

Bejel, Emilio. 2001. *Gay Cuban Nation*. Chicago: Chicago University
Press.

———. 2009. "José Martí: Iconografía y memoria." *La Habana Elegante*.
Accessed November 27, 2009. http://www.habanaelegante.com/Fall
_Winter_2009/Invitation_Bejel.html.

Benjamin, Walter. 1969a. "On Some Motifs in Baudelaire." In *Illuminations*, edited by Hannah Arendt and translated by Harry Zohn, 187–
88. New York: Schocken Books.

———. 1969b. "The Work of Art in the Age of Mechanical Reproduction." In *Illuminations*, edited by Hannah Arendt and translated by
Harry Zohn, 217–51. New York: Schocken Books.

———. 1999a. "Franz Kafka: On the Tenth Anniversary of His Death."
In *Selected Writings*, edited by Michael W. Jennings, vol. 2, 794–818.
Cambridge: Belknap.

―――. 1999b. "Little History of Photography." In *Selected Writings*, edited by Michael W. Jennings, vol. 2, 507–30. Cambridge: Belknap.

Berger, John. 2003. "Photographs of Agony." In *The Photography Reader*, edited by Liz Wells, 288–90. New York: Routledge.

Bermúdez, Jorge R. 1990. "Martí y la fotografía." *Bohemia* 29 (June): 92–94.

―――. 1999. "Evolución de la imagen pictórica y gráfica de José Martí." *Debates Americanos* 7–8:47–57.

―――. 2004. *Antología visual José Martí en la plástica y la gráfica cubanas*. Havana: Editorial Letras Cubanas.

Bosteels, Bruno. 2010. "Marx y Martí: Lógicas del desencuentro." *Nómada*, 63–73. Accessed March 10, 2011. http://www.scribd.com/doc/47973904/Marx-y-Marti-logicas-del-desencuentro-Bruno-Bosteels.

Brown, Wendy. 2003. "Resisting Left Melancholia." In *Loss: The Politics of Mourning*, edited by David Eng and David Kazanjian, 458-65. Berkeley and Los Angeles: University of California Press.

Bronze Gallery. n.d. "Anna Hyatt." Accessed September 15, 2011. http://www.bronze-gallery.com/sculptors/artist.cfm?sculptorID=75.

Butler, Judith. 1997. *The Psychic Life of Power*. Stanford: Stanford University Press.

Camacho, Jorge. 2003. "Los herejes en el convento: La recepción de José Martí en la plástica y la crítica cubana de los años 80 y 90." *Espéculo: Revista de estudios literarios* 24. Accessed September 15, 2008. http//www.ucm.es/info/especulo/numero24/herejes.html.

Carricarte, Arturo R. 1925. *Iconografía del Apóstol José Martí*. Havana: Secretaría de Instrucción Pública y Bellas Artes.

Casero, Luis. 1995. "Carta al editor." *Diario de las Américas*, July 6.

Castro, Fidel. 1975. *History Will Absolve Me*. Translated by Pedro Álvarez Tabío and Andrew Paul Booth. Havana: Editorial de Ciencias Sociales.

Daumont, Lysbeth. 2011. "Con José Martí ante la mar tempestuosa." *Opus Habana*, January 28.

De la Fuente, Alejandro. 2001. *A Nation for All: Race, Inequality, and Politics in Twentieth-Century Cuba*. Chapel Hill: University of North Carolina Press.

Del Valle, Rufino. 2004–5. "Cuba, sus inicios fotográficos." *Opus Habana* 3, 8:415. Reproduced in *Habananuestra*, September 26, 2009, 1.

Dettman, Jonathan. Forthcoming. "Writing after History: Essays on the Post-Soviet Cuban Novel." PhD diss., University of California–Davis.

Diario de la Marina. 1951. July 1.

Doane, Mary Ann. 2007. "The Indexical and the Concept of Medium Specificity." *Differences: A Journal of Feminist Cultural Studies* 18, 1:128–52.

Duttlinger, Carolin. 2008. "Imaginary Encounters: Walter Benjamin and the Aura of Photography." *Poetics Today* 29, 1:79–101.

Eng, David, and David Kazanjian, eds. 2003a. *Loss: The Politics of Mourning.* Berkeley and Los Angeles: University of California Press.

———. 2003b. "Introduction: Mourning Remains." In *Loss: The Politics of Mourning,* edited by David Eng and David Kazanjian, 1-25. Berkeley and Los Angeles: University of California Press.

Ette, Ottmar. 1994. "Imagen y poder—poder de la imagen: Acerca de la iconografía martiana." In *José Martí 1895 / 1995: Literatura – Política – Filosofía – Estética,* 223–97. Frankfurt: Vervuert Verlag.

Fernández Retamar, Roberto. 1969. "Modernismo, noventiocho, subdesarrollo." In *Ensayo de otro mundo,* 52–62. Santiago, Chile: Editorial Universitaria.

———. 1978. *Introducción a José Martí.* Havana: Casa de las Américas and Centro de Estudios Martianos.

———. 2006. "Martí, Lenin y la revolución anticolonial." In *Camino a lo alto: Aproximaciones marxistas a José Martí,* edited by Lourdes Pasalodos, 66–89. Havana: Editorial de Ciencias Sociales.

Font, Mauricio F., and Alfonso W. Quiroz, eds. 2006. *The Cuban Republic and José Martí: Reception and Use of a National Symbol.* Oxford: Lexington Books.

Fountain, Anne. 2003. *José Martí and U.S. Writers.* Gainesville: University Press of Florida.

Freud, Sigmund. 1900. *The Interpretation of Dreams.* In *Standard Edition of the Complete Psychological Works of Sigmund Freud,* edited and translated by James Strachey, vols. 4 and 5. London: Hogarth Press and the Institute of Psycho-Analysis.

———. 1953–74. "Fetishism." In *Standard Edition of the Complete Psychological Works of Sigmund Freud,* edited and translated by James Strachey, vol. 21, 147-58. London: Hogarth Press and the Institute of Psycho-Analysis.

———. 1954. *The Origins of Psycho-Analysis: Letters to Wilhelm Fliess, Drafts and Notes, 1887–1902.* Edited by Marie Bonaparte, Anna

Freud, and Ernst Kris. Translated by Eric Mosbacher and James Strachey. London: Imago.

————. 1955. "The Ego and the Id." In *Standard Edition of the Complete Psychological Works of Sigmund Freud*, edited and translated by James Strachey, vol. 19, 1-59. London: Hogarth Press and the Institute of Psycho-Analysis.

————. 1974. "Mourning and Melancholia." In *Standard Edition of the Complete Psychological Works of Sigmund Freud*, edited and translated by James Strachey, vol. 14, 239-60. London: Hogarth Press and the Institute of Psycho-Analysis.

Galería Cubarte. n.d. "Andrés González González." Accessed December 22, 2011. http://www.galeriacubarte.cult.cu/g_artista.php?item=124&lang=sp.

————. n.d. "José Villalta Saavedra." Accessed February 21, 2009. http://www.galeriacubarte.cult.cu/g_artista.php?item=70&lang=sp.

————. n.d. "Juan José Sicre." Accessed August 3, 2007. http://www.galeriacubarte.cult.cu/g_artista.php?item=72&lang=sp.

————. n.d. "Mario Santi." Accessed April 13, 2009. http://www.galeriacubarte.cult.cu/g_artista.php?item=80&lang=sp.

García Canclini, Néstor. 1989. *Culturas híbridas: Estrategias para entrar y salir de la modernidad.* Mexico City: Grijalba.

Gonçalves, Joáo Felipe. 2006. "The 'Apostle' in Stone: Nationalism and Monuments in Honor of José Martí." In *The Cuban Republic and José Martí: Reception and Use of a National Symbol*, edited by Mauricio A. Font and Alfonso W. Quiroz, 18–33. New York: Lexington Books.

————. 2007. "Nationalism and the City: Havana and Miami, 1959–1990." International Dissertation Research Fellowships of the Social Science Research Council. Accessed January 10, 2011. http://programs.ssrc.org/idrf/Fellows/2007/Goncalves/.

————. 2010. "Identity and the Politics of Memory in the Cuban Diaspora: Monuments to José Martí in Miami, 1959–1995." Videotaped lecture delivered on February 22. 46 minutes. YouTube. Accessed November 24, 2011. http://vimeo.com/9652720.

González Echevarría, Roberto. 2002. "José Martí: An Introduction." In *José Martí: Selected Writings*, edited by Esther Allen, ix–xxv. New York: Penguin Books.

Guerra, Lillian. 2005. *The Myth of José Martí: Conflicting Nationalisms in Early Twentieth-Century Cuba*. Chapel Hill: University of North Carolina Press.

———. 2006. "The Struggle to Redefine Martí and 'Cuba Libre' in the 1920s." In *The Cuban Republic and José Martí: Reception and Use of a National Symbol*, edited by Mauricio A. Font and Alfonso W. Quiroz, 34–50. New York: Lexington Books.

Gutiérrez Alea, Tomás. 1966. *La muerte de un burócrata*. Havana: ICAIC.

Halbwachs, Maurice. 1980. *The Collective Memory*. Translated by Francis J. Ditter Jr. and Yida Yazdi Ditter. New York: Harper and Row.

Hall, Stuart. 2003. "Pensando en la diáspora: En casa, desde el extranjero." In *Heterotopías: Narrativas de identidad y alteridad latinoamericana*, edited by Carlos A. Jáuregui and Juan Pablo Dabove, 477–500. Pittsburgh: Instituto Internacional de Literatura Iberoamericana.

Hannabach, Cathy. 2010. "Photographic Traces and Cinematic Returns: Review of Garrett Stewart's *Framed Time*." *Time & Society Review of Books* 19:154–57.

Harris, Alex. 2007. *The Idea of Cuba*. Durham: Center for Documentary Studies at Duke University.

Hart Dávalos, Armando. 2006. "Martí y Marx, raíces de la revolución socialista de Cuba." In *Camino a lo alto: Aproximaciones marxistas a José Martí*, edited by Lourdes Pasalodos, 324–53. Havana: Editorial de Ciencias Sociales.

Hernandez-Reguant, Ariana, ed. 2009a. *Cuba in the Special Period: Culture and Ideology in the 1990s*. New York: Palgrave Macmillan.

———. 2009b. "Writing in the Special Period: An Introduction." In *Cuba in the Special Period: Culture and Ideology in the 1990s*, edited by Ariana Hernandez-Reguant, 1–18. New York: Palgrave Macmillan.

Hernández Serrano, Luis. 2009. "Los fotógrafos de José Martí." *Cubaperiodistas.cu*. Accessed June 9, 2010. http://www.upec.cu/marti _periodista/37.htm.

Huyssen, Andreas. 1995. *Twilight Memories: Marking Time in a Culture of Amnesia*. London: Routledge.

Jameson, Fredric. 1988. "Cognitive Mapping." In *Marxism and the Interpretation of Culture*, edited by Cary Nelson and Lawrence Grossberg, 347–57. Champaign: University of Illinois Press.

Jelin, Elizabeth. 2002. *Los trabajos de la memoria*. Madrid and Buenos Aires: Siglo XXI Editores.

Jrade, Cathy L. 1998. *Modernismo, Modernity, and the Development of Spanish American Literature.* Austin: University of Texas Press.

Kirk, John M. 1983. *José Martí: Mentor of the Cuban Nation.* Gainesville: University Press of Florida.

Kunzle, David. 1997. *Che Guevara: Icon, Myth, and Message.* Los Angeles: UCLA Fowler Museum of Cultural History and the Center for the Study of Political Graphics.

"La Fragua Martiana." n.d. In Ecu Red. Accessed December 23, 2011. http://www.ecured.cu/index.php/Fragua_Martiana.

Lacan, Jacques. 2004. "The Function and Field of Speech and Language in Psychoanalysis." In *Écrits: A Selection,* translated by Bruce Fink, Héloïse Fink, and Russell Grigg, 31–106. New York: W. W. Norton.

Lazzara, Michael. 2009. "Pinochet's Cadaver as Ruin and Palimpsest." In *Telling Ruins in Latin America,* edited by Michael Lazzara and Vicky Unruh, 121–34. New York: Palgrave Macmillan.

López, Alfred J. 2006. *José Martí and the Future of Cuban Nationalisms.* Gainesville: University Press of Florida.

Mañach, Jorge. 1950. *Martí: Apostle of Freedom.* Translated by Coley Taylor. New York: Devin-Adan.

———. 1968. *Martí el apóstol.* Madrid: Espasa Calpe.

Marinello, Juan. 2006. "El caso literario de José Martí." In *Camino a lo alto: Aproximaciones marxistas a José Martí,* edited by Lourdes Pasalodos, 41–65. Havana: Editorial de Ciencias Sociales.

Martí, José. 1975a. "Coney Island." *Obras completas* 9:123–28.

———. 1975b. "The Memorial Meeting in Honor of Karl Marx." Translated by Philip S. Foner. In *Inside the Monster: Writings on the United States and American Imperialism,* edited by Philip S. Foner, 184–88. New York: Monthly Review Press.

———. 1975c. "El Poema del Niágara." *Obras completas* 7: 222–38.

———. 1975d. *Obras completas,* vols. 1–27. Havana: Editorial de Ciencias Sociales.

———. 1869. "Abdala." *La Patria Libre.*

———. 1881. "Progreso inmenso." *La Opinión Nacional,* January.

———. 1884. "Una fotografía es un revólver." *La América,* May.

———. 1885. "¡Los fotógrafos poblarán el mundo!" *La Opinión Nacional,* January.

———. 2002. "Prologue to Juan Antonio Pérez Bonalde's *Poem of Niagara*." In *José Martí: Selected Writings*, edited by Esther Allen, 43–51. New York: Penguin Books.

Martín-Barbero, Jesús. 1987. *De los medios a las mediaciones*. Mexico City: Gustavo Gili.

Martínez, Higinio. 1895. "Muerte de Martí." Havana: *La Caricatura*, June 95. Reproduced in Oller Oller, "Historia de las fotos que corroboraron la muerte de José Martí," 2010.

Martínez-Echazábal, Lourdes. 1991. "'Martí and the Race': A Re-Evaluation." In *Re-Reading José Martí (1853–1895): One Hundred Years Later*, edited by Julio Rodríguez-Luis, 115–26. Albany: State University of New York Press.

Martínez Estrada, Ezequiel. 1967. *Martí revolucionario*. Prologue by Roberto Fernández Retamar. Havana: Casa de las Américas.

Masiello, Francine. 2009. "Scribbling on the Wreck." In *Telling Ruins in Latin America*, edited by Michael Lazzara and Vicky Unruh, 27–38. New York: Palgrave Macmillan.

McAndlish, Phillips. 1965. "Statue of Cuban Finally Placed." *New York Times*, April 20.

Mead Jr., Robert G. 1965. "Letter to the Editor of the Times," May 26.

Mella, José Antonio. 2006. "Glosas al pensamiento de José Martí." In *Camino a lo alto: Aproximaciones marxistas a José Martí*, edited by Lourdes Pasalodos, 12–19. Havana: Editorial de Ciencias Sociales.

Merleau-Ponty, Maurice. 1968. *The Visible and the Invisible*. Edited and translated by Claude Lefort. Evanston: Northwestern University Press.

Metz, Christian. 1990. "Photograph and Fetish." In *The Critical Image: Essays on Contemporary Photography*, edited by Carol Squiers, 155–64. Seattle: Bay Press.

Mirabal, Nancy Raquel. 1995. "'Más que negro': José Martí and the Politics of Unity." In *José Martí in the United States: The Florida Experience*, edited by Louis A. Pérez, Jr., 57–69. Tempe: Arizona State University Center for Latin American Studies.

Mitchell, W. J. T. 1986. *Iconology: Image, Text, Ideology*. Chicago and London: University of Chicago Press.

———. 2003. "Benjamin and the Political Economy of the Photograph." In *The Photography Reader*, edited by Liz Wells, 53–58. London: Routledge.

——. 2005. "There Are No Visual Media." *Journal of Visual Culture* 4:257–66.

——. 2006. *What Do Pictures Want?: The Lives and Loves of Images*. Chicago: University of Chicago Press.

Molloy, Sylvia. 1992. "Too Wilde for Comfort: Desire and Ideology in Fin-de-Siecle Spanish America." *Social Text* 31–32:187–201.

Monsiváis, Carlos. 1995. *Los rituales del caos*. Mexico City: Ediciones ERA.

Montero, Oscar. 2004. *José Martí: An Introduction*. New York: Palgrave Macmillan.

Morán, Francisco. 2007. "'Sueño con claustros de mármol': Homo-heroísmo o la veta en el mármol de la escritura martiana." *Mandorla*: 345–71.

New York Times. 1960. "Central Park Ceremony for Cuban Hero Erupts into Riots over Castro." January 29, 5.

——. 1965a. "City Unveils Statue of Martí on Tuesday." May 16, 52.

——. 1965b. "Disputed Statue of Cuban to Go Up: City Will Put José Martí Figure in Central Park after 13-Year Wait." January 27, 37.

——. 1965c. "Martí's Statue Unveiled after a 7-Year Wait." May 19, 49.

——. 1965d. "Statue of Cuban Hero out in Open." April 3, 31.

——. 1965e. "Statue of Cuban Finally Placed." April 20, 41.

——. 1965f. "City Unveils Statue of Martí on Tuesday." May 16, 52.

Noble, Andrea. 2005. "Photography, Memory, Disavowal: The Casasola Archive." In *Images of Power: Iconography, Culture and the State in Latin America*, edited by Jens Andermann and William Rowe, 195–216. New York: Berghahn Books.

Nora, Pierre. 1989. "Between Memory and History: *Les lieux de mémoire (1984)*." *Representations* 26:7–25.

Oller Oller, Jorge. 1984. "1841. La Habana se retrata por primera vez." *Granma*, September 29. Quoted in *Cubaperiodistas.cu*, September 5, 2008.

——. 2008. "La primera fotografía informativa y la primera crítica." *Cubaperiodistas.cu*, September 5.

——. 2010a. "El primer fotógrafo que retrató a los cubanos." *Cubaperiodistas.cu*, December 29.

————. 2010b. "Historia de las fotos que corroboraron la muerte de José Martí." In *Manejo y gestión de centros históricos*, June 4. Accessed May 30, 2011. cubaperiodistas.cu/fotorreportaje/48.html.

Peirce, Charles S. 1932. *Writings of Charles S. Peirce: A Chronological Edition*, vol. 1. Bloomington: Indiana University Press.

Pérez, Louis A. 1988. *Cuba: Between Reform and Revolution*. New York: Oxford University Press.

Quesada y Miranda, Gonzalo. 1985. *Iconografía martiana*. Havana: Editorial Letras Cubanas.

Radstone, Susannah, ed. 2000a. *Memory and Methodology*. Oxford: Berg.

————. 2000b. "Working with Memory: An Introduction." In *Memory and Methodology*, edited by Susannah Radstone, 1–22. Oxford: Berg.

————. 2000c. "Screening Trauma: *Forrest Gump*, Film and Memory." In *Memory and Methodology*, edited by Susannah Radstone, 79–107. Oxford: Berg.

Rama, Ángel. 1995. *La ciudad letrada*. Montevideo, Uruguay: Arca.

————. 1996. *The Lettered City*. Translated and edited by John Charles Chasteen. Durham: Duke University Press.

Ramos, Julio. 1989. *Desencuentros de la modernidad en América Latina: Literatura y Política en el siglo XIX*. Mexico City: Fondo de Cultura Económica.

Ripoll, Carlos. 1984. *José Martí, the United States, and the Marxist Interpretation of Cuban history*. New Brunswick: Transaction Books.

————. 1994. "The Falsification of José Martí in Cuba." *Cuban Studies* 24:3–38.

————. 1995. *La vida íntima y secreta de José Martí*. New York: Editorial Dos Ríos.

Rodríguez-Luis, Julio, ed. 1991. *Re-Reading José Martí (1853–1895): One Hundred Years Later*. Albany: State University of New York Press.

Rojas, Rafael. 2000. *José Martí: La invención de Cuba*. Madrid: Ediciones Colibrí.

————. 2006. "'Otro gallo cantaría': Essay on the First Cuban Republicanism." In *The Cuban republic and José Martí: Reception and Use of a National Symbol*, edited by Mauricio A. Font and Alfonso W. Quiroz, 7–17. New York: Lexington Books.

————. 2008a. *Motivos de Anteo: Patria y nación en la historia intelectual de Cuba*. Madrid: Editorial Colibrí.

———. 2008b. "*Orígenes* and the Poetics of History." In *Essays in Cuban Intellectual History*, 65–91. New York: Palgrave Macmillan.

———. 2008c. *Essays in Cuban Intellectual History*. New York: Palgrave Macmillan.

Santí, Enrico Mario. 1986. "José Martí and the Cuban Revolution." *Cuban Studies* 16:139–50.

———. 1995. "Pensar a José Martí." *Diario de las Américas*. May 20:12.

———. 1996. *Pensar a José Martí: Notas para un centenario*. Boulder: Society of Spanish and Spanish-American Studies: 1–9.

———. 1999. "Thinking Through Martí." In *Re-Reading José Martí (1853–1895): One Hundred Years Later*, edited by Julio Rodríguez-Luis, 67–83. Albany: State University of New York Press.

Scarpaci, Joseph L., Roberto Segre, and Mario Coyula, eds. 2002. *Havana: Two Faces of the Antillean Metropolis*, revised edition. Chapel Hill: University of North Carolina Press.

Schulman, Ivan. 1966. *Génesis del modernismo: Martí, Nájera, Silva, Casal*. Mexico City: El Colegio de México and Washington University Press.

Schulman, Ivan A., and Manuel Pedro González. 1969. *Martí, Darío y el modernismo*. Madrid: Editorial Gredos.

Scribner, Charity. 2003. "Left Melancholia." In *Loss: The Politics of Mourning*, edited by David Eng and David Kazanjian, 300–19. Berkeley and Los Angeles: University of California Press.

Stewart, Garrett. 2007. *Framed Time: Toward a Postfilmic Cinema*. Chicago: University of Chicago Press.

Talese, Gay. 1964. "Cubans Fail in Attempt to Place Martí Statue: Exiles Find Plaster Model Too Heavy to Lift to Pedestal." *New York Times*, October 10.

Tejada, Roberto. 2009. *National Camera: Photography and Mexico's Image Environment*. Minneapolis: University of Minnesota Press.

Vitier, Cintio, and Fina García Marruz. 1981. *Temas martianos*. Río Piedras, Puerto Rico: Ediciones Huracán.

Weiss, Rachel. 2011. *To and from Utopia in the New Cuban Art*. Minneapolis and London: University of Minnesota Press.

Wells, Liz, ed. 2003. *The Photography Reader*. London: Routledge.

Whyld, Bea. 2005. "Anna Hyatt Huntington and the Huntington Great Danes." *Subrosa*, 42. Accessed September 15, 2011. http://huntingtonbotanical.org/Rose/Subrosa/42/annahyatt.htm.

Williams, Susan S. 1996. "'The Inconstant Daguerreotype': The Narrative of Early Photography." *Narrative* 2, 4: 161–74.

Winter, Jay. 2010. "Sites of Memory." In *Memory: Histories, Theories, Debates*, edited by Susannah Radstone and Bill Schwarz, 312–24. New York: Fordham University Press.

Wollen, Peter. 2003. "Fire and Ice." In *The Photography Reader*, edited by Liz Wells, 76–86. London: Routledge.

Wood, Nancy. 1999. *Vectors of Memory: Legacies of Trauma in Postwar Europe*. Oxford: Berg.

Index

Page numbers in boldface refer to figures or tables.